Essays and Studies 1993

The English Association

The object of the English Association is to promote the knowledge and appreciation of English language and literature.

The Association pursues these aims by creating opportunities of co-operation among all those interested in English; by furthering the recognition of English as essential in education; by discussing methods of English teaching; by holding lectures, conferences, and other meetings; by publishing a journal, books, and leaflets; and by forming local branches overseas and at home.

Publications

The Year's Work in English Studies. An annual bibliography. Published by Blackwell (U.S.A.: Humanities Press).

Essays and Studies. An annual volume of essays by various scholars assembled by the collector covering usually a wide range of subjects and authors from the medieval to the modern. Published by D. S. Brewer.

English. The journal of the Association, *English* is published three times a year by the Association.

Newsletter. A *Newsletter* is published three times a year giving information about forthcoming publications, conferences, and other matters of interest.

Benefits of Membership

Institutional Membership

Full members receive copies of *The Year's Work in English Studies*, *Essays and Studies*, *English* (three issues) and three *Newsletters*.

Ordinary Membership covers *English* (three issues) and three *Newsletters*.

Schools Membership includes two copies of each issue of *English*, one copy of *Essays and Studies*, three *Newsletters*, and preferential booking and rates for various conferences held by the Association.

Individual Membership

Individuals take out Basic Membership, which entitles them to buy all regular publications of the English Association at a discounted price, and attend Association gatherings.

For further details write to The Secretary, The English Association,
The Vicarage, Priory Gardens, London W4 1TT.

Essays and Studies 1993

Literature and Censorship

**Edited by
Nigel Smith**

for the English Association

D. S. BREWER

ESSAYS AND STUDIES 1993
IS VOLUME FORTY-SIX IN THE NEW SERIES
OF ESSAYS AND STUDIES COLLECTED ON BEHALF OF
THE ENGLISH ASSOCIATION
ISSN 0071–1357

First published 1993 by D. S. Brewer, Cambridge

D. S. Brewer is an imprint of Boydell & Brewer Ltd
PO Box 9, Woodbridge, Suffolk IP12 3DF, UK
and of Boydell & Brewer Inc.
PO Box 41026, Rochester, NY 14604, USA

ISBN 0 85991 387 2

British Library Cataloguing-in-Publication Data
Literature and Censorship. – (Essays &
Studies Series, ISSN 0071–1357;Vol.46)
I. Smith, Nigel II. Series
363.310941
ISBN 0–85991–387–2

The Library of Congress has cataloged this serial publication:
Catalog card number 36–8431

211969

This publication is printed on acid-free paper

Printed in Great Britain by
St Edmundsbury Press Ltd, Bury St Edmunds, Suffolk

Contents

Preface

Censorship has recently attracted much attention. 'Censorship is a notion of extraordinary potency. Through it we define ourselves as readers, writers, and as citizens,' writes Neil Sammells in his introduction to *Writing and Censorship in Britain* (Routledge, 1992), eds. Sammells and Paul Hyland (p. 13). The Rushdie affair is an instance of a shrinking world, where the proximity of very different cultures with differing views of toleration becomes decidedly uncomfortable. In the literary west, we live (so we think) free from the fear of violent censorship and repression that exists in many other parts of the world. Crucial to our sense of history is the belief that our literature had been involved in a struggle against different forms of repressive authority. Victory (however partial it may seem to some) in that struggle is usually assumed to be one guarantee of a tolerant society, and a major factor in the richness of English literature.

Yet attitudes to censorship can change. Do not religions other than Christianity deserve legal protection from defamation, just as an 'enlightened position' claims the right to inflict censorship on harmful and backward attitudes? That censorship might be a strategy for achieving a common good, that the legal paraphenalia of toleration might be a form of political control itself, that censorship of personal morality and sexual behaviour might inevitably be involved in the very production of that which it attempts to suppress – these insights urge us to think again.

Rather than censorship being a tyrannical evil, gradually erased in the histories of the most progressive societies, we are nowadays more likely to think of it as an important aspect of the power relations which permeate a society. It is a tool not only of rulers, and, as far as literature is concerned, censorship matters most in the connection of an author's private realm of speculation to the public sphere of shared values. If censorship is part of power, and belongs to a greater or lesser degree, to all, we can more easily and interestingly link public and official censorship to those private forms of censorship which occur before publication, and (the particular interest of psychoanalysis) before the pen meets the page, or in the act of composition itself. The study of censorship is not a subcompartment of publishing history: it reaches into every aspect of literary interpretation.

The essays in this volume are all concerned with this relationship, and they each develop an unexpected aspect of the behaviour of censorship in literature. Richard Wilson's study of *A Midsummer Night's Dream* shows how Shakespeare encodes the conditions of his own freedom of expression in the play, linking this with the play's equally half-hidden portrayal of social control in 1590s England. The 'dream' for the mechanicals is a use of the theatre in which they dare to threaten their rulers, and Shakespeare's play is seen as an acute questioning of a tacit compromise between authors and authority: how far could you go to risk hanging?

Where for Shakespeare, authorship and censorship interact to induce creative plenitude, the conditions of relative press freedom in the 1640s created an anxiety of authorship for Milton. Lucasta Miller's essay shows how Milton and his pamphlet enemies accustomed themselves to printed battle. Press freedom to debate the Word of God facilitated the birth of the printed author, but it also meant the death of the orator or preacher. Being unable to control your text, because it was subject to mutilation and distortion in the hands of an opponent, induces an anxiety which 1640s pamphleteers were unable to dispel. Similarly, Paul Hammond's essay demonstrates 'uncensorship': once freed from the author's control, Restoration manuscript poetry was made more politically controversial or sexually salacious by revision when in manuscript circulation – a testimony to the capacity of manuscripts (as opposed to print) to transmit and develop unlicensed opinion in the early modern period.

Jonathan Bate's essay adds the matters of forgery and authenticity to censorship in the field of cultural politics in the 1790s. Edmond Malone's exposure of William Henry Ireland's forged Shakespeare manuscripts was in fact part of the political battlefield of the 1790s. Both Ireland and Malone were in the business of presenting Shakespeare selectively, that is to say, of censoring Shakespeare's text. If Malone exposed a fraud, Ireland revealed in Malone the manufacturing of a Tory Shakespeare.

Jon Mee's article is an example of the analysis of actual censorship of which we are much in need. The allegorical 'bricolage' literature of 1790s popular radicals was designed to evade or frustrate the seditious libel legislation of 1792, itself meant to effect the suppression of such literature. Mee is able to show how radical views were expressed in the very act of evading the censor, simultaneously luring a censoring authority onto the spikes of undecidable legal interpretation, and hence defeat in court.

The personal and the social are brought together in Joseph

Bristow's detailed reading of Rossetti's 'Jenny'. The poet's denial of a voice for Jenny exemplifies the Victorian male's anxiety concerning the attractiveness, the shame, and the exploitation of the prostitute. Yet, argues Bristow, the poem is neither oppressive of its subject, nor repressive of the poet's or the speaker's self, nor emancipatory through its art. Rather, the disjuctions of 'Jenny' bluntly disclose the sexual politics which have brought them about, and the silence in the poem is an invitation to understand the forces that have made it.

Likewise, Kate Flint argues that Virginia Woolf's refusal to name lesbian sexual practices and feelings in her novels (unlike her private letters) allows the reader a freedom to explore the questions which are suggested but not fixed by the novelist. It is no coincidence that Milton's works display the threat of the female *and* the public arena of print to the author, whereas Woolf uses the public space of the novel to challenge gender conventions, and, of course, the notion of the author.

Martin Wiggins returns the collection to issues of public power by showing how one act of censorhsip by a government-funded body, the BBC, depended upon the personal reaction of the most powerful person in the institution. Indeed, the Director of Programmes at the BBC seems to have been placed as a viewer by Dennis Potter's television play as a viewer in very much the same position as Rossetti's young man: at the conjunction of moral and sexual standards then at the centre of public debate. Horrified and made decidedly uncomfortable by the suggestions disclosed in the play (for the viewer is forced to identify with the devil), the response of the Director was a banishment (at least for several years) of the play from the medium for which it was intentionally written.

The focus of the essays in this collection moves from the simultaneous apprehension of governing power and private fantasy on the Renaissance stage through the negotiation of freedom of expression (and its effects) in publishing, to the troubling of the sexual economy and gender boundaries by the author's use of censorship, and finally to the question of public intervention in the most domestic space of artistic consumption, the suburban sitting room. As a body, the essays represent a number of new ways of thinking about censorship. There seems, at least as yet, to be no fixed view of what censorship might be: rather it is a protean set of relationships by which the most personal kinds of desire and expression and the politics of the community at large have negotiated with each other. If our society has become more tolerant, it has also begun to be more comprehending of the matter of fact that all kinds of expression are involved in this negotiation. At a time of blunt government interference in national and educational culture, this reminder is more than apt.

Yet we should not forget that censorship is in many places a matter of life and death, of torture and immense suffering, as a perusal of any issue of the *Index on Censorship* will confirm. The Civil Rights Movement of Sri Lanka recently started to publish a series entitled 'Values in Dissent'. The first issue is a pamphlet anthology of various materials published in the belief that 'progress depends on the free exchange of conflicting ideas', a truly Miltonic statement. Sri Lanka has experienced sustained civil unrest in recent years, including widespread killings and persecutions of innocent and uninvolved citizens by partisan forces. In response, the Civil Rights Movement determined to 'keep certain civil values alive, . . . to promote understanding not only of the right to dissent, but also of the intrinsic value of dissent'. To this end, it envisages a programme of publishing writings made in the name of dissent, records of discoveries made through dissent, and accounts of relevant legal decisions. The first issue contains statements by E.M. Forster and Stephen Spender, extracts from *King Lear*, prison letters by Adam Michnik, and an article on the Victorian Dr John Snow's pioneering but slow-to-be-accepted work on cholera contraction. There is a colonial question here (why should Sri Lankans read so much English literature?), but the collection is nonetheless stirring, and one that strongly associates the writing and reading of sophisticated imaginative literature with the well-being of a free society. We should be in no doubt that literature is a good force in a troubled world. To this end, we must hope that after bad censorship comes good private censorship and public negotiation.

The Kindly Ones: The Death of the Author in Shakespearean Athens

RICHARD WILSON

WHENEVER KARL MARX CONTEMPLATED British politics he was reminded of *A Midsummer Night's Dream*, and when he considered Britain's token opposition he thought of the bathetic mew of Snug the Joiner. Victorian parliamentarians who imagined themselves as earth-shakers, he joked, were like Shakespeare's craven craftsman, unconvincingly acting out the rage of the British lion; while the thunder of a *Times* editorial was a charade to which the only possible response was Demetrius's ironic applause for Snug's fox-like valour: 'Well roar'd lion!' The secret of British compromise, Marx inferred, was contained in the discretion with which the workers and nobles defer to each other in Shakespearean Athens; and if modern France had gone from revolutionary tragedy to constitutional comedy, this was because Napoleon III had learned from Duke Theseus to manage politics 'as a masquerade in which grand costumes, words, and postures serve only as masks,' and the Paris mob played its part 'as Nick Bottom plays that of the lion,' *sotto voce* and roaring 'as gently as any sucking dove' (I, ii, 87). After 1848, Marx considered, conservative rule throughout Europe was 'like the lamentable comedy of Pyramus and Thisbe performed by Bottom and his friends': a pitiful burlesque. History repeats itself the second time as farce in a parliamentary system, he deduced, because sovereignty and subversion are both neutralised in the synthesis that is predicted in Shakespeare's play: 'It is like the lion in *A Midsummer Night's Dream*, who calls out: "I am a lion!" and then whispers "I am not a lion, but only Snug". Thus every extreme is at one time the lion of contradiction, at another the Snug of mediation.'[1] Representing bloody tragedy as a comic game, therefore, parliament tames the revolution; and if Shakespeare remained,

This essay was first given as a lecture at Leeds University in December 1992, and I am grateful to Dr Martin Butler for playing Philostrate on that occasion. All quotations of Shakespeare are from the Arden editions.

[1] Quoted in S.S. Prawer, *Karl Marx and World Literature* (Oxford, 1976), pp. 58, 168, 179, 242, 244, 246.

as Eleanor Marx reported, her father's Bible,[2] that was in part because of the uncanny way in which the plot of A *Midsummer Night's Dream* seemed to him to premonitor this historic reversal.

The lion who did not dare to roar was an Aesopian figure, according to Marx, for the British culture of consensus. He noticed, that is to say, that the headpiece worn by Snug has meta-dramatic significance in Shakespeare's comedy, like the face of the choric actor in Greek tragedy which carried the caption, 'I advance behind my mask.' For the Duke who commands a performance of 'very tragical mirth' from the 'Hard-handed men that work in Athens . . . Which never labour'd in their minds till now' (V, i, 57; 72–3), is, indeed, the prototypical Shakespearean prince: in his wisdom that power requires circuses and that far from being set against authority, theatricality is, in Stephen Greenblatt words, 'one of power's essential modes.'[3] As Thomas Nashe explained when the aldermen objected to playhouses in 1592, the English monarchy could learn from what the actor told Augustus, the 'patron of all witty sports,' when 'there happened a great fray in Rome about a player . . . Whereupon the Emperor . . . called the player before him, and asked why a man of his quality durst presume to make a quarrel about nothing. He smilingly replied: 'It is good for thee, O Caesar, that the people's heads are troubled with brawls about our light matters; for otherwise they would look into thee and thy matters.'[4] In an essay on the Stuart fashion for classical plays, Martin Butler confirms that what drew dramatists to the ancient world was precisely the seriousness with which rulers took the 'airy nothing' of theatre (V, i, 16) when legendary 'Roscius was an actor in Rome' (*Hamlet*, II, ii, 389); so it is significant that Shakespeare's *Dream* has been connected with a wedding on February 19 1596 in the family of the official most identified with such patronage, the Lord Chamberlain, Lord Hunsdon.[5] For the antics of Julius Caesar, who makes 'the

2   Quoted, ibid., p. 356.

3   S. Greenblatt, 'Invisible Bullets: Renaissance Authority and its Subversion, *Henry IV* and *Henry V*', in R. Dutton and R. Wilson (eds.), *New Historicism and Renaissance Drama* (London, 1992), p. 98.

4   T. Nashe, 'Pierce Penniless', in *The Unfortunate Traveller and other works*, ed. J.B. Steane (Harmondsworth, 1972), p. 115: 'A Player's Witty Answer to Augustus'.

5   M. Butler, 'Romans in Britain: *The Roman Actor* and the Early Stuart Classical Play', in D. Howard (ed.), *Philip Massinger: A Critical Reassessment* (Cambridge, 1985), pp. 139–70. The association of A *Midsummer Night's Dream* with the wedding of Elizabeth, daughter of Sir George Carey and

tag-rag people . . . clap and hiss him . . . as they use to do the players in the theatre' (*Julius Caesar*, I, ii, 255–8), are prefigured by this Duke of Athens when he likewise plots with his Master of Revels to legitim- ate the violence of his empire with triumphal games:

> Go Philostrate,
> Stir up the Athenian youth to merriments;
> Awake the pert and nimble spirit of mirth;
> Turn melancholy forth to funerals;
> The pale companion is not for our pomp.
> Hippolyta, I woo'd thee with my sword,
> And won thee doing thee injuries;
> But I will wed thee in another key,
> With pomp, with triumph, and with revelling.   (I, i, 12–19)

Though Bacon scorned such 'masques and triumphs' as 'but toys,'[6] a shift in humanist thinking on public entertainment is detectable in Montaigne, who admired Demosthenes for avoiding 'all magnificence' in 'parades of athletes and festivals,' yet recognised the awesome power of the amphitheatre, 'where you could seat a hundred thousand men,' under a system where 'authority depended (in appearance at least) on the will of the people.'[7] The marble O of the ancient circus might provide panoptic discipline for a modern town, as the professors of Vicenza demonstrated when they built their semi-globular *Teatro Olimpico* in 1584. Likewise, it was Olympic Greece which in 1612 inspired Midland landowners to sponsor their Cotswold Games as an antidote to peasant revolt.[8] And Theseus, who despite impatience

granddaughter of Henry, Lord Hunsdon, and Thomas, son of Lord Berkeley, was proposed by Peter Alexander in *Shakespeare's Life and Art* (London, 1939), p. 105; supported by Harold Brooks in the Arden edition of the play (London, 1979), pp. lvi–lvii, and is now generally accepted. For Hunsdon's defence of the players, see R. Dutton, *Mastering the Revels: The Regulation and Censorship of English Renaissance Drama* (London, 1991), pp. 105–6.

6 F. Bacon, 'Of Masques and Triumphs', in *Essays*, ed. M.J. Hawkins (Lon- don, 1973), p. 115.

7 M. Montaigne, 'On coaches', in *The Complete Essays*, trans. M.A. Screech (London, 1991), pp. 1021, pp. 1024–6.

8 For the *Teatro Olimpico*, see D.J. Gordon, 'Academicians Build a Theatre and Give a Play', in *The Renaissance Imagination* (Berkeley and London, 1972), pp. 247–68; and for the Cotswold Olympics, see C. Whitfield, ed., *Robert Dover and the Cotswold Games: Annalia Dubrensia* (Evesham, 1962); and D. Brailsford, *Sport and Society: Elizabeth to Anne* (London, 1969), pp. 103–16. Dover's Games, like Theseus's, incorporated a traditional fixture,

with 'antique fables' and 'fairy toys' (V, i, 3), revives the defunct Midsummer custom of gadding through the 'quaint mazes in the wanton green' (II, i, 99), seems to personify this neoclassical strategy, with his Platonist scheme to 'find the concord' in the discord of his subjects through the 'music' of race meetings and the office of his 'usual manager of mirth' (IV, i, 105; V, i, 60). His marriage to the Amazonian Queen would literally provide a key of pomp and circumstance with which to harmonise family, church and royalty when set to Mendelssohn's march; but in the meantime it would offer a programme for the manufacture of consensus by monarchs such as James I, whose *Book of Sports* and triumphal entry into London inaugurated a true 'theatre state'.[9] Yet if this Duke is exemplary for Shakespeare's later rulers in commemorating his wedding with an amnesty to 'overbear' the 'ancient privilege of Athens' and pardon sexual crimes (I, i, 41; IV, 178), their duplicity in the taverns of Eastcheap and brothels of Vienna casts suspicion on his motive when he likewise despatches an *agent provocateur* downtown to 'stir up' the delinquent to misrule. For Shakespeare's Athens has an underworld like London's, we infer, and magistrates who have devised the blueprint for a metropolitan police.

'Turn melancholy forth to funerals': there is no place in this Athens for a Don John, Jacques, or Malvolio, and the banishment of the malcontent that closes later comedies here initiates the plot. Yet ever since Jan Kott exposed a diabolical underside to Shakespeare's *Dream*, with its 'slimy, hairy, sticky creatures' that arouse 'violent aversion,'[10] critics have interpreted this tactic as a psychological repression, and it has become a commonplace that 'if death is officially absent from our play . . . indications of its proximity abound.'[11] Thus, Louis Montrose traces a cycle of sexual violence throughout the text emanating from

where Page's greyhound had been 'outrun' in 1597 (*The Merry Wives*, I, i, 82–92).

9 For the *Book of Sports* as an ideological instrument, see L. Marcus, *The Politics of Mirth: Jonson, Herrick, Milton, Marvell, and the Defense of Old Holiday Customs* (Chicago, 1986), passim. The concept of the 'theatre state' is derived from the seminal study of Clifford Geertz, *Negara: The Theatre State in Nineteenth-Century Bali* (Princeton, 1980).

10 J. Kott, 'Titania and the Ass's Head,' in *Shakespeare Our Contemporary* (London, 1965), p. 182.

11 R. Girard, 'Sweet Puck! Sacrificial Resolution in A *Midsummer Night's Dream*', in A *Theater of Envy: William Shakespeare* (Oxford, 1991), p. 239.

its Ovidian sources and patriarchal dread of female power;[12] and René Girard sees a scapegoat ritual in which blood sacrifice is deflected by Puck from its intended victims, the feuding boys, Demetrius and Lysander.[13] This anthropological criticism merges with an old historicism which has long speculated that the play is an allegorical mirror to reflect the crisis of the 1590s, and that Titania's report on the ruined harvest refers specifically, as the Arden editor deduced, to the calamitous dearth of 1595–7 (II, i, 88–114).[14] What these readings share is a belief that the play is structured according to the looking glass logic of an actual dream, and that the method in its madness is the metonymic dream-work decoded by that Freudian analyst, Mercutio, when he observes how lovers always dream of kisses; courtiers, curtsies; lawyers, fees; and soldiers, 'cutting foreign throats' (*Romeo and Juliet*, I, iv, 70–88). Whatever the critic, then, there is respect for Hippolyta's intuition that 'all the story of the night told over . . . More witnesseth than fancy's images' (V, i, 23–5); and a sense that this 'talking cure' abreacts desires and anxieties which shadow the play in fantasies of rape and murder, and fears of those 'jaws of darkness' that gape in 'Sickness, war, or death' (I, i, 142–8). Exiled at the start, the 'pale companion' returns by night, to haunt those 'crossways' where the hanged are buried with the unconscious of the text (III, ii, 383).

'What a dream was here! . . . Methought a serpent ate my heart away' (II, ii, 148): like that 'green and gilded snake' that coils about the sleeping Oliver in *As You Like It* (IV, iii, 109), Hermia's nightmare belongs to a pastoralism that insists on the coincidence of desire and death: *Et in Arcadia Ego*.[15] And from the instant when the Duke

---

[12] L. Montrose, 'A *Midsummer Night's Dream* and the Shaping Fantasies of Elizabethan Culture', in Dutton and Wilson (note 3), pp. 109–30.

[13] Girard, op. cit. (note 11). For Girard's anthropological theory of literature as sacrifice, see also *Violence and the Sacred*, trans. P. Gregory (Baltimore, 1977); see especially pp. 104–8 for the sacrifice of the king in animal form.

[14] H.F. Brooks, ed., *A Midsummer Night's Dream: The Arden Shakespeare* (London, 1979), pp. xxxvi–xxxviii.

[15] For the Neoplatonist hermeneutics of the 'concealed God' and a reading of Shakespeare's comedy as a coded text, see R. Cody *The Landscape of the Mind: Pastoralism and Platonist Theory in Tasso's 'Aminta' and Shakespeare's Early Comedies* (Oxford, 1969), pp. 127–150. For pastoralism and the convention of the *momento mori*, see E. Panofsky, '*Et in Arcadia Ego*: Poussin and the Elegiac Tradition', in *Meaning and the Visual Arts* (London, 1970); and for the messenger of death in the comedies, see especially A. Barton, '*As You Like It and Twelfth Night*: Shakespeare's Sense of an ending', in M. Bradbury

sentences her 'Either to die the death, or to abjure for ever the society of men' for loving Lysander (I, i, 65–6), *A Midsummer Night's Dream* stages the tension of the condemned, suspended between a verdict and reprieve. Under the sign of the scaffold, then, this solstice is passed in 'fog, as black as Acheron,' the river of Hades, conjured by the 'king of shadows,' Oberon (III, ii, 347–56). What many critics perceive, however, is that the threat of death to which the lovers subject themselves by their desires is sublimated in the *Lamentable Comedy and Most Cruel Death of Pyramus and Thisbe* presented by the mechanicals, which travesties both Ovid's tragic story and the *Liebestod* of *Romeo and Juliet*. There the Bacchic blood which dyed the mulberry a lurid 'deep dark purple colour' in Golding's *Metamorphoses* is dissolved into the narcotic 'juice' of that 'little western flower . . . now purple with love's wound,' which seems, when Puck lays it 'on sleeping eyelids,' to emblematise the toxicity of Shakespeare's own Aesculapian art (II, i, 166–70). Metonymy and condensation, rather than metaphor and displacement, govern this author's dreaming, we observe, which functions not as an antidote but as a poison. Moreover, Girard further notices a sinister similarity between the three alternative dramas offered for performance to Theseus, which all involve 'something that vainly attempts to force its way' into the *Dream*, but is 'everywhere on the periphery, marginal, excluded, yet unmistakably present': namely, the brutal scapegoating of a poet:[16]

> [Reads] 'The battle with the Centaurs, to be sung
> By an Athenian eunuch to the harp'?
> We'll none of that; that I have told my love,
> In glory of my kinsman Hercules.
> [Reads] 'The riot of the tipsy Bacchanals,
> Tearing the Thracian singer in their rage'?
> That is an old device, and it was play'd
> When I from Thebes came last a conqueror.
> [Reads] 'The thrice three Muses mourning for the death
> Of learning, late deceas'd in beggary'?
> That is some satire, keen and critical,
> Not sorting with a nuptial ceremony.   (V, i, 44–55)

and D. Palmer (eds.), *Stratford-upon-Avon Studies, 14: Shakespearean Comedy* (London, 1972), pp. 160–80.
16 Ovid, *Metamorphoses*, trans. A. Golding (London 1567; repr. London, 1961), IV: 152, p. 85. Girard, op. cit. (1991, note 11), p. 240.

Emasculation, dismemberment, oblivion: in all three tragedies, Girard comments, 'a poet happens to be the victim. In the first he is castrated; in the second, lynched. In the third, he dies alone, abandoned by all. This last is the modern way of doing things.'[17] From the Greek castrato and the martyred Orpheus, to the destitute genius in a garret, whom scholars identify as Robert Greene, snuffed out by poverty in 1592, Philostrate's repertoire flatters his prince with the progress of censorship from mutilation of the body to enlightened neglect. Shakespeare would revert to the savage spectacle of the violent death of the author in *Julius Caesar*, when the poet Cinna meets the fate of Orpheus at the hands of the Thracian women, as the mob shouts to 'Tear him to pieces . . . Tear him for his bad verse!' (III, iii, 28–30). Later in the same play, however, we also observe the modern practice, when another Poet is mocked by the subjects of his satire for the 'vileness' of his 'cynic rhyme' (IV, iii, 132); and in Athens it seems there is doubt about which form of censorship applies. The Duke runs a line through *The Death of Learning* with the wariness of one who knows how 'the poet's pen . . . gives to airy nothing / A local habitation and a name' (V, i, 15–17), but defends the suppression on aesthetic grounds. In a patronage system, we see, literary criticism is superseding torture as the more subtle means of cultural control; yet the first concern of Peter Quince when his actors receive their parts is that he will suffer like Orpheus if their performance similarly makes 'the ladies . . . shriek: and that were enough to hang us all.' Francis Flute's fear of sharing the embarrassment of the Athenian eunuch, when he is effeminised as Thisbe, testifies to the same panic about a catastrophic loss of voice; and the rendition of *Pyramus and Thisbe* stutters on Nick Bottom's solemn confirmation that 'if you should fright the ladies out of their wits, they would have no more discretion but to hang us' (I, ii, 70–6). Evidently the Maenads still menace this Renaissance court.

'That would hang us, every mother's son': the players' anxiety about how 'the Duchess and the ladies' will respond (70–3) is given weight by official reaction in 1597 to the play called *The Isle of Dogs*, when the actors and the part-author, Ben Jonson, were imprisoned in the Marshalsea for performing 'very seditious and slanderous matter.'[18]

---

[17] Ibid.
[18] C.H. Herford and P. Simpson, *Ben Jonson: Life and Works*, Vol. 1 (Oxford, 1925), pp. 15–16. See Dutton, op. cit. (note 5), pp. 107–10 for an authoritative account of the issues raised by *The Isle of Dogs* episode.

None of the text survives, but the title implies an Aesopian fable such as that which doomed the last Englishman executed for seditious libel, William Collingbourne, hanged in 1484 'for making a foolish rhyme' about Richard III and his ministers, Catesby, Ratcliffe and Lovell, which ran: 'The Cat, the Rat, and Lovell the Dog / Do rule all England, under a Hog.' According to the poet, the meaning of this doggerel 'was so plain, that every fool perceived it'; and Annabel Patterson comments that his mistake had indeed been to breach a tacit compromise between English authors and authority, whereby each knew 'how far a writer could address contemporary issues' in code, 'so that nobody would be *required* to make an example of him.'[19] Likewise, John Stubbs had the hand cut off which penned an over-explicit squib on the Queen in 1579; but the compact was also liable to be broken by the state, as was shown in 1633, when William Prynne lost his ears for libelling the King, despite his plea that he 'had no ill intention . . . but may be ill interpreted.'[20] Quince's worries belong to the period between these verdicts analysed by Richard Dutton, when government insecurity led to a nervy inconsistency towards topical material, such as the deposition of Richard II played on the eve of Essex's rebellion in 1601, as the Queen noted, '40 times in open streets and houses'. Though no Elizabethan actors were hanged or mutilated for libel, as Philip Finkelpearl points out, they were right to be apprehensive about such a system, which might one day tolerate them and the next haul them before the judges, as Shakespeare's colleagues were on that occasion.[21] For even this most 'puzzling incident of noncensorship'[22] revealed the Damoclean justice under which theatre functioned.

If critics are polarised between those who stress the reluctance of

---

[19] For Collingbourne's case, see A. Patterson, *Censorship and Interpretation: The Conditions of Writing and Reading in Early Modern England* (Madison, Wis., 1984), pp. 12–13.

[20] Stubbs had written *The Discovery of a Gaping Gulf whereinto England is like to be Swallowed* as a warning against Elizabeth marrying the Duke of Alençon; see Dutton, op. cit. (note 5), p. 59. Prynne quoted in Patterson, op. cit. (note 19), p. 107; for a discussion of his case, see Chap. 2.

[21] See P. Ure, ed., *Richard II: The Arden Shakespeare* (London, 1966), p. lix. For a review of conflicting theories concerning the *Richard II* incident, see Dutton, op. cit. (note 5), Chap. 5.

[22] P.J. Finkelpearl, 'The Comedians' Liberty: Censorship of the Jacobean Stage Reconsidered', *English Literary Renaissance*, 16 (1986), p. 124; Patterson, op. cit. (note 19), p. 17.

the censors, and others, such as Jonathan Dollimore, who insist that 'dramatists *were* imprisoned and harassed by the State for staging plays,'[23] this divide is a measure, Dutton argues, of the Janus-face of Renaissance theatrical authority; and it is an ambiguity that troubles Shakespeare's text. For when Bottom demands to know 'What is Pyramus? A lover, or a tyrant?' he raises doubts about how to represent power to the powerful and whether the Duke will prove 'condoling' like a lover or imitate his cousin 'Ercles'. . . tyrants' vein' (I, ii, 19–36). It had been as Hercules that Caesar notoriously took to the boards, and 'carried away with the violence' of the role, slew an actor 'dead at his feet, and after swung him (as the poet said) about his head'; so Bottom's 'humour' to play the tyrant and 'make all split' (25) is tempting fate.[24] The 1598 Vagrancy Act would indeed ordain penalties of whipping and death for unlicensed playing; and Quince's eagerness to modulate his actors' frenzy reflects a genuine attempt to forestall such confusion of reality with fiction. Though critics are right, then, to view these scenes as indicative of 'how the play speaks to itself, in a surreptitious voice,' of its conditions of production, they underestimate the dangers in 'the unforseeable consequences . . . of getting the ladies over-excited.'[25] Like *Julius Caesar*, *A Midsummer Night's Dream* is a play about poetry and power, and how they read each other, and the trap Quince is so desperate to avoid is precisely the hermeneutic circle which had made ancient theatre so lethal, when stage-struck Caesars projected themselves into the parts of tyrants, regardless of the stock disclaimer that if the characters portrayed put anyone 'in remembrance of things past, / Or things intended, 'tis not in us to help it.'[26] In 1604 Chapman, Jonson and Marston would risk having 'their ears cut and noses' for offending the

[23] J. Dollimore, *Radical Tragedy: Religion, Ideology and Power in the Drama of Shakespeare and his Contemporaries*, rev. ed. (Hemel Hempstead, 1989), p. 24.
[24] For an account of this famous (though probably apocryphal) episode and the representational questions raised, see J. Drakakis, 'Fashion it Thus: *Julius Caesar* and the Politics of Theatrical Representation', in *Shakespeare Survey*, 41 (1990), pp. 65–6.
[25] J.H. Kavanagh, 'Shakespeare in ideology', in J. Drakakis, ed., *Alternative Shakespeares* (London, 1985), pp. 154–5. The operation of the 1598 Act is discussed in Dutton, op. cit. (note 5), pp. 110–11.
[26] P. Massinger, *The Roman Actor*, I, iii, 139–40, in P. Edwards and C. Gibson, eds, *The Plays and Poems of Philip Massinger* (Oxford, 1976), III, p. 33. See also Butler, op. cit. (note 5).

King in *Eastward Ho!*;[27] but Quince knows the best apology for actors before an audience whose intentions are so hard to read is a Delphic periphrasis:

> If we offend, it is with our good will.
> That you should think, we come not to offend,
> But with good will. To show our simple skill,
> That is the true beginning of our end.
> Consider then, we come but in despite.
> We do not come, as minding to content you,
> Out true intent is.　　　　　　　　　　　　(V, i, 108–14)

Shakespeare's *Dream* is 'contaminated', Montrose writes, by the legends of Theseus's tyranny, which it recycles to engender further 'violence, fear and betrayal . . . for it shapes the fantasies by which it is shaped, begets that by which it is begotten.'[28] There can be no escape, for this New Historicist reading, from the violence of representation; but what such paranoia misses is a deeper *anxiety* of representation, and the dream-like process the play rehearses whereby nightmare scenarios are revised. For the classical canon is constantly edited in Shakespeare's comedy, which proceeds through a series of rejected scripts. Seneca's *Hercules*, Euripides' *Bacchae*, above all, Ovid's *Metamorphoses*, are all evaded during the action as potential endings of a plot that seems, instead of impasse, to seek a way out of the textual labyrinth, as Theseus led the young from that 'wood of Crete' (IV, i, 112), and its human monster, in a different myth. Rather than shaping struggle, culture is here the thing which struggle shapes, and the most typical cultural act is the redaction the players undertake when Bottom objects that 'There are things in this comedy of Pyramus and Thisbe that will never please,' and Tom Snout agrees that since 'the ladies cannot abide' to see a sword, 'we must leave the killing out, when all is said and done'. Bottom's solution, to 'put them out of fear' with a prologue 'to say we will do no harm with our swords,' would appear, in fact, to have extra-dramatic status as a statement of authorial intention to dilute Ovidian blood (III, i, 8–21). Likewise, the rewriting to entreat the Ladies 'not to fear, not to tremble' at the Lion, on the understanding that he is 'no such thing' but 'a man, as other men are,' (40–3) seems designed so as not to 'let

---

27 Herford and Simpson, op. cit. (note 18), p. 38.
28 L. Montrose, op. cit. (note 12), pp. 121 and 130.

Aesop fable' on this summer's night (3 *Henry VI*, V, v, 25). Thus, far from perpetuating a cycle of violence, the disingenuousness of this author is to deny his own affectivity, with a contract that stakes everything not on sharing, but on renouncing power, as Bottom bargains with the Ladies: 'my life for yours!' (40).

What is an author? An author, Foucault observes, is not, as we imagine, the origin of meaning, but rather, 'the principle by which, in our culture, one limits, chooses, and impedes the circulation of fiction . . . a figure for our fear of the proliferation of meaning.' Books and discourses began to have authors, Foucault explains, 'to the extent that authors became subject to punishment.' Renaissance writing was therefore fraught with risk; but from the Shakespearean period, according to this account, a penal system of censorship gave way to an authorial system of ownership, as texts which previously circulated anonymously were validated only when endowed with names. Henceforth the censor could relax to the degree that authors took upon their own heads responsibility for their words, allowing us 'to ask of each fictional text: From where does it come, who wrote it, when, under what circumstances, or with what design?'[29] It is this responsibility which seems to be staged in the *Dream*, when Quince translates the fable into his own iambic pentameter, composes Pyramus's prologue and Lion's apology, interpolates Moonshine and Wall, cuts the warring parents, and writes 'Bottom's Dream'. . . to be sung in the latter end of the play' (IV, i, 212–6). Unlike King Claudius, then, Theseus does not need to ask his Master of Revels, 'Have you heard the argument? Is there no offence in it?' (*Hamlet*, III, ii, 227–8), because the author has censored himself and followed the advice of James I, to 'beware of writing anything on the commonwealth or such subjects, except metaphorically,' since these matters were 'too grave for a Poet to mell in.'[30] For the effect of his revision is to render management redundant when the Master hears his mirth, and to reduce his source, as the minister says, to an innocuous 'nothing, nothing in the world' (V, i, 77–8). The privileges of an author begin, we see, at the point when literature retreats from 'the world' of referentiality into the empty 'nothing' of its own aesthetic void:

[29] M. Foucault, 'What is an Author?' in P. Rabinow, ed., *The Foucault Reader: An Introduction to Foucault's Thought* (Harmondsworth, 1984), pp. 109, 118.
[30] Quoted in Patterson, op. cit. (note 19), p. 20.

All for your delight,
We are not here. That you should here repent you,
The actors are at hand; and by their show,
You shall know all, that you are like to know.   (V, i, 114–17)

If Shakespeare avoided the pains of authorship through such self-effacement, this was by a design we must distinguish, as Leah Marcus remarks, from innocence of intention; and sweet Quince, whose 'small Latin' is such an obstacle to his love of Ovid, can indeed be seen as a 'humble alter ego' of the author whose own Ovidian style earned him his reputation as 'honey-tongued'.[31] So, if this carpenter who so rapidly writes, casts, costumes, equips, revises, rehearses, and stages his play by royal command, is Shakespeare's self-portrait, then the *Dream* can be compared to pictures of the artist in his studio, such as *Las Meninas* (*The Waiting Women*) by Velazquez, which is another representation where representation 'undertakes to represent itself,' in Foucault's words, 'in all its elements, with its images, the eyes to which it is offered, the faces it makes visible, the gestures that called it into being.'[32] For in this portrait the Baroque painter depicted himself working in a similar *métier*, beside the ladies and dwarfs of the court, who pass judgement on his canvass, as he gazes out of the frame to a place hypothetically occupied by his models, who are dimly reflected, peering from a mirror at the back, as the King and Queen, positioned where we, the spectators, in fact stand. 'The entire picture is looking out at a scene for which it is itself a scene';[33] so, like the *Dream*, this is a work that describes a moment when art cuts itself free from the world to which it refers, but is obliged by its terms of production to restore that world as compliment to a prince. For if the mirror functions in the painting like the play within the play, both presuppose that they depend on one who cannot be presented, because of

[31] L. Marcus, *Puzzling Shakespeare: Local Reading and its Discontents* (Berkeley, Calif., 1988), pp. 40–1. For Francis Meres's 1598 commendation of Shakespeare as the English Ovid see S. Schoenbaum, *William Shakespeare: A Documentary Life* (Oxford, 1975), pp. 139–42. See also A.B. Taylor, 'Golding's Ovid, Shakespeare, 'Small Latin', and the real object of the mockery in *Pyramus and Thisbe*', in *Shakespeare Survey*, 42 (1991), pp. 60–4.
[32] M. Foucault, *The Order of Things: An Archaeology of the Human Sciences*, trans. anon. (London, 1974), p. 16. In the background of Velazquez's picture there is also a mysterious 'pale companion', who stands, framed in the door, giving the lie to the mirrored illusion of the King and Queen.
[33] Ibid., p. 14.

occupying, paradoxically, the centre stage. In each, this ghostly figure is the patron on whom everything depends; for Shakespeare, 'the imperial votress,' Queen Elizabeth, who passes by in the realm of anecdote, unseen except as a pale reflection (II, i, 163), putative spectator of a play that hinges, as Montrose remarks, not 'upon her presence or intervention, but, on the contrary, her absence, her exclusion.'[34]

Quince calculates that 'to bring moonlight into a chamber' is one of theatre's 'hard things,' and can only be done through a glass darkly, as Bottom suggests throwing the shutters of 'the great chamber window, where we play, open; and the moon may shine in at the casement' (III, i, 45–54). So, if this moon who spies through windows as she pretends a 'maiden meditation, fancy-free' (II, i, 164), is, as editors presume, a refraction of Elizabeth in her guise as Diana, the technical problem of presenting moonshine seems metonymic of the difficulty of representing power on the Renaissance stage. As they quiz the almanac to find whether 'the moon doth shine that night we play,' the actors acknowledge the queen of the night as a presiding genius, but Robin Starveling's effort 'to disfigure . . . the person of Moonshine' with 'a bush of thorns and a lantern' is ludicrous as an illusion of majesty. Any literal attempt to 'find out moonshine' is bound to be frustrated (III, i, 48–57); and this is lucky, because the moon is throughout invested with ominous repressive powers. She is the 'fruitless moon' (I, i, 73), 'the cold moon' (II, i, 156), 'the wat'ry moon' (II, i, 162), 'the wand'ring moon' (IV, i, 98), the 'governess of floods' whose frigid emotions cause disaster, as, 'Pale in her anger [she] washes all the air, / That rheumatic diseases do abound. / And thorough this distemperature we see / The seasons alter' (II, i, 103–7). Above all, this moon is old and tired, her days numbered from the start: 'but O, methinks, how slow / This old moon wanes! She lingers my desires, / Like to a stepdame or a dowager / Long withering out a young man's revenue' (I, i, 3–6). The whole community waits upon this dying heiress, longing for 'the next new moon,' whose masculine succession, 'like to a silver bow, / New bent in heaven,' will bring mercy to his subjects and marriage to the court (I, i, 83; 9); but the impudence of this image of the haggard crone with her hoard of jewels makes it improbable that Gloriana was present in that 'great chamber' in Blackfriars when the Dream was first performed.

Editors notice a discrepancy in Shakespeare's plot, which promises

[34] Montrose, op. cit. (note 12), p. 125.

that 'four happy days bring in / Another moon' and 'the night of our solemnities' (I, i, 2–11), but which accelerates to the wedding next day. Moreover, since Oberon and Titania are 'ill met by moonlight' on their way to 'moonlight revels', and Quince rehearses 'by moonlight', the old moon is still in the sky on Midsummer night, and is again seen, by Puck, after midnight at the end of the second day (II, i, 60, 141; I, ii, 95; V, i, 358). Neither new moon nor the moonless night preceding it comes as expected in *A Midsummer Night's Dream*, which closes with the 'horned moon' still 'withering out' her end (232–5). If this moon is like the mirror in the painting, then, and reveals a face of power that cannot be presented on stage, Shakespeare's almanac must tabulate the uncertain political conjunction it records, which the critics maintain was that of the hungry summer of 1595, when 'the ox stretch'd his yoke in vain, / The ploughman lost his sweat, and the green corn … rotted ere his youth attain'd a beard' (II, i, 93–5). 'The husbandman perceiveth that the new moon maketh plants and creatures fruitful,' recorded Reginald Scot in 1584, 'but decaying in the wane,' and that 'One born in the spring of the moon shall be healthy; in the time of the wane, when the moon is utterly decayed, the child cannot live.'[35] Mention of the lunar cycle is a reminder, therefore, of the belief that, as governess of menstruation and tides, a waning moon brought blood, tears, sterility and death, so that, as John Aubrey warned, 'it is not good to undertake any business at the last period of her revolution.'[36] 'Swear not by the moon, th'inconstant moon,' Juliet had cautioned Romeo, 'That monthly changes in her circled orb' (*Romeo and Juliet*, II, ii, 109–110); and the aged moon of Shakespeare's *Dream* does resemble the worn-out face that looked down in 1595 on a world of 'pacts and sects' whose greatness ebbed with hers (*King Lear*, V, iii, 18–19).

In the autumn of her *annus horribilis*, when Shakespeare began his play about dreams and divinations, the Queen was not expected to live long; but the author superstitiously avoided looking for the new moon through the window of his text. Likewise, custom counselled caution when he gestured at the declining planet, since it was reckoned 'unlucky to point at the moon,' lest you became her

[35] R. Scot, *The Discovery of Witchcraft* (London, 1584), IX, ii and iii, quoted in I. Opie and M. Tatem, eds., *Oxford Dictionary of Superstitions* (Oxford, 1992), p. 260.
[36] J. Aubrey, *Remains* (London, 1881), p. 85, quoted ibid., p. 261.

prisoner, like the Man in the Moon.[37] When the moon climbs on stage, framed by the play within the play, the smoking candle Moonshine swings in his lantern comes as near to satire, then, as any actor dared. 'All I have to say,' mumbles Starveling, 'is, to tell you that the lantern is the moon; I the Man i'th'Moon; this thorn-bush my thorn-bush; and this dog my dog' (V, i, 247-9); and if his pantomime seems nonsensical, this is because it parodies the symbols of masques with which Elizabeth was regaled. 'If we had thought so much would have been said of us,' she rasped after one such charade on November 17, where Essex acted out his love, 'we would not have come down tonight,' and so went back to bed.[38] With the Man in the Moon, however, the players circumvented the taboo on royal allusion, since this most 'ancient and popular superstition' tells of a 'poor man which stole a bundle of thorns' for firewood, and was punished by being 'set into the moon, there for to abide for ever'. 'The face of the man in the moon,' according to folklore, 'is the face of a man who went hedging';[39] so, Starveling is living up to his name when he mimes one of the most militant rites of social protest: breaking of fences, trespass, and theft of wood. No wonder the Duke quips that 'the man should be put in the lantern,' for this was the custom that gave a name to the radicalism of 'the plain people of London' who would call themselves the Levellers.[40] Or that the courtier should so relish the gallows humour when he condemns the actors: 'Why, all these should be in the lantern' (237-50). The shadow that crosses the moon at this joke is that of a noose, for the dictionary reminds us that in Tudor slang to be 'in the lantern' meant to be hanged from the post.

'Marry, if he that writ it had . . . hang'd himself . . . it would have been a fine tragedy' (343-6): Theseus's verdict gives the last twist to a chillingly self-reflexive game in which Shakespeare tempts judgement. For his moon is like the artist's mirror in reflecting not only his

[37] Ibid., pp. 264 and 282-3.
[38] G.B. Harrison, *The Life and Death of Robert Devereux, Earl of Essex* (London, 1937), p. 91.
[39] J. Brand, *Observations on the Popular Antiquities of Great Britain* (London, 1849), III, p. 476; Opie and Tatem, op. cit. (note 34), p. 264.
[40] Leveller pamphlet quoted in P. Burke, 'Popular Culture in Seventeenth Century London', in B. Reay (ed.), *Popular Culture in Seventeenth-Century England* (London, 1988). p. 51. Burke points out that a number of the leading Levellers were playwrights or actors; and for the London origins of the movement, see also D. Underdown, *Revel, Riot and Rebellion: Popular Politics and Culture in England, 1603-1660* (Oxford, 1985), p. 213.

play, but the absent presence beyond, where Elizabeth's 'small light' was 'already in snuff' as Starveling's candle guttered 'in the wane' (240–4). At the end Puck will carefully sweep such 'wasted brands' away; but at this moment the superstitious might read the future in 'the dead and drowsy fire' (360–78); as a London servant foretold the Queen's eclipse and a new king from her kitchen fire in 1595. On June 6 this prophecy was proclaimed at Mansion House by a weaver who made 'hard speeches' against the government and predicted a land of plenty when Elizabeth died. Assuming him to be mad, the Mayor committed him to Bedlam, from where he was rescued, however, by a mob of apprentices, who began to realise his dream by erecting a gibbet outside the Mayor's door and raiding the market stalls for butter and fish. And when the organisers of this price fixing were arrested, citizens attacked the prison and set them free. Altogether, there were a dozen riots in London during the Midsummer season preceding Shakespeare's play, an outburst of fury against food shortage historians describe as the 'most dangerous urban uprising' between the accession of the Tudors and the Civil War.[41] The climax came on June 29, when a thousand artisans fought the militia on Tower Hill, cheered by troops from the Tower, whose Governor was subsequently discovered to have plotted to install the Earl of Hertford as king.[42] So strong were the Earl's expectations of succession that the Governor was never tried; but on July 4 martial law was declared, and

[41] Historic Manuscripts Commission, *Salisbury Papers*, V, 248–50; IX, p. 191; *Calendar of State Papers Domestic, 1595–7*, p. 82; BL. Landsdowne MS. 78, nos. 64–5 (ff. 159–61); R. Manning, *Village Revolts: Social Protest and Popular Disturbances in England, 1509–1640* (Oxford, 1988), p. 208. See also P. Williams, *The Tudor Regime* (London, 1979), pp. 329–30.

[42] See R. Manning, 'The Prosecution of Sir Michael Blount, Lieutenant of the Tower of London, 1595', in *Bulletin of the Institute of Historical Research*, 57 (1984), pp. 216–24. A.F. Pollard's theory in DNB. that Hertford (Edward Seymour) and his henchmen escaped prosecution for treason because of court support, including his kinsman Hunsdon's, for the Earl's claim to the crown, may explain why *A Midsummer Night's Dream* was able to sail so close to the wind. Hoping to secure her nomination, Hertford staged the Entertainment at Elvetham for the Queen in 1591, which Chambers saw as a source for Oberon's reminiscence of Cupid's abortive 'love-shaft' at 'the watery moon' (II, i, 155–64); and after the Midsummer imbroglio of 1595 he was investigated by Lord Cobham: Hunsdon's rival and successor as Lord Chamberlain, whose family was Shakespeare's presumed butt in *The Merry Wives* (see E.K. Chambers, *Shakespearean Gleanings* (London, 1946), pp. 63 f.; and Dutton, op. cit. (note 5), pp. 102–5).

under its terms six craftsmen were drawn on hurdles through the streets and hanged. Shakespeare's Midsummer tableau, with the starving tailor as the Man hanging from the gallows in the sky, seems, in the circumstances, a mute paraphrase of the 'moonshine' of the Queen's Peace.

Peter Quince, joiner; Nick Bottom, weaver; Francis Flute, bellows mender; Tom Snout, tinker; Snug, joiner; Robin Starveling, tailor: the cast list of the lamentable comedy played in Athens reads, in the light of the Midsummer nightmare of 1595, like the indictment of a conspiracy trial. And it is easy to imagine what a prosecutor would make of the activities of this 'crew of patches [and] rude mechanicals, / That work for bread upon [the city's] stalls,' who plot to trespass 'in the palace wood, a mile without the town, by moonlight,' under cover of a seasonal mumming traditionally acted under 'the Duke's oak' (I, ii, 94–102; III, ii, 9–10). Once met, these masterless men assign themselves aliases, disguise themselves with masks, false beards, and women's clothes, and debate whether to 'leave the killing out' or 'do harm' with their swords, before they depute one of their number to 'enter into the brake' deep in the park wearing animal skin, and on a given 'cue', 'steal' from the estate as much 'provender' of cereals, meat, and liquor as he can (III, i, 71; IV, i, 199, 31), while the others keep up a riotous noise of rough music on 'the tongs and the bones' (29). Questioned by magistrates, the main offender justifies his crimes with a 'ballad' in which he claims to have been under the orders of the Queen of the Fairies, who had promised him the Land of Cockaigne (213). The ringleader's defence, that he had been incited to misrule by a high official, will cut no ice against such self-incriminating evidence; for in fact this case is one that will recur at assizes in late medieval and early modern England, when two opposing concepts of justice clash, as they do in London in 1595, and the old calendar customs that sanctioned lawlessness run up against new rules of property and profit. In particular, it will be at Midsummer and the feast of Corpus Christi that the Whitsun game of free-for-all, with its rites of trespass and disguise, will carry its players into violent conflict with authority; such as that which occurred in Kent on Midsummer Night 1451, when:

William Cheeseman, yeoman; Tom Crudd, husbandman; John Jope, yeoman; Jack Nash, sadler; Dick Peek, butcher; Will Stone, labourer; with others unknown, in riotous manner and arrayed for war with breastplates, halberds, bows and arrows . . . and covered with long beards and painted on their faces with black charcoal, calling themselves the servants of the Queen of the Fairies, intending that their names should not be known, broke into the park of Humphrey, Duke of Buckingham, at Penshurst, and chased, killed and took away from the said park 10 bucks and 72 does belonging to the said Duke, against the King's Peace and the statute of parks lately issued.[43]

Like the gang who cut down the hedges of Windsor Park in 1607 under pretext of Shrovetide football, the Penshurst fairies were acting out a hallowed scenario of resistance. 'And these are not fairies?' asks the victim of one such 'skimmington', Sir John Falstaff, after he has been mugged under Herne's Oak, 'I was three or four times in the thought they were not fairies.' Shakespeare knew that English fairies were likely to be the footballers of towns like Windsor, and that the Fairy Queen would turn out, as she does in *The Merry Wives*, to be a citizen 'Finely attired in a robe of white' (IV, iv, 70; V, v, 121–2). Fairyland had been secured by Jack Cade's rebels in 1450, when they too dubbed their hero 'Queen of the Fairies.'[44] So, when Bottom is 'translated' to the 'fairy kingdom' in the Duke's park (III, i, 114; II, i, 144), he treads a well-known 'maze' into the world of popular politics (99), where his hunger is sure to be relieved. For fairies were seen as agents of folk justice, according to Keith Thomas, who enforced charity and hospitality, and the appeal to their Queen was a recall to collective values.[45] Theologians even imagined them old-style Catholics, as Richard Corbet fancied: 'since of late, Elizabeth, / And after, James, came in, / They never danced on any heath, / As when the time hath been. / By which we note the Fairies were of the old profession, / Their songs were Ave Maries, / Their dances were procession.'[46] But if Queen Mab was as Marian as Mercutio also hints, her moral economy was that of the real 'little people': the peasants and craftsmen. Thus, Jonson saw her as 'She, that pinches country wenches / If they rub not clean their benches, / And with sharper nails remembers, / When they rake not up the embers'; and Thomas

[43] F.R.J. Du Boulay, ed., *Kent Records: Documents illustrative of medieval Kentish Society*, Kent Archaeological Society (Ashford, 1964), pp. 254–5.

[44] R. Flenley, *Six Town Chronicles* (London, 1911), p. 127.

[45] K. Thomas, *Religion and the Decline of Magic: Studies in popular beliefs in Sixteenth and Seventeenth Century England* (Harmondsworth, 1973), pp. 724–34.

[46] R. Corbett, 'The Fairies' Farewell', lines 29–36, in *Poems of Richard Corbett*, ed. J.A.W. Bennett and H.R. Trevor Roper (Oxford, 1955), pp. 49–52.

notes that fairy law was retributive if not propitiated: 'They might reward benefactors, but if neglected would avenge,' for fairies were both good and evil.[47] In the *Dream* this dualism of punishment and reward is fought out in the nocturnal war between Oberon and Titania for their adopted heir, but it is focused in Puck, the 'merry wanderer' who tramples 'over park and over pale' (II, i, 4; 43) unless correctly pacified, he:

> That frights the maidens of the villagery,
> Skim milk, and sometimes labour in the quern,
> And bootless make the breathless housewife churn,
> And sometimes make the drink to bear no barm,
> Mislead night-wanderers, laughing at their harm.
> Those that Hobgoblin call you, and sweet Puck,
> You do their work, and they shall have good luck.   (34–41)

'Those that Hobgoblin call' him, or 'sweet Puck,' or 'that shrewd and knavish sprite / Call'd Robin Goodfellow' (33–4), know what's in a name, for 'Modo he is called, and Mahu,' philologists note, since his name is legion who can never be named: Old Nick, Satan, the Devil, who is also, sometimes, Oberon. 'The Prince Darkness is a gentleman,' we believe (*King Lear*, III, iv, 140), as long as he is addressed respectfully, for what matters is *how* he is spoken to. Thus, Carlo Ginzburg has described the folk religion of north-east Italy in the 1590s as premised on 'night battles' for control of the crops, which were fought by 'wanderers' who called the powers of darkness by a name they gave themselves: the *benandanti*, or 'goodfellows'.[48] The logic of this homeopathic magic is, of course, that of the *pharmakon* – the poison that cures – which Derrida sees as language's repression of its Other; so it is no coincidence that Shakespeare's Fairies have optimistic names from folk pharmacy: Cobweb, Moth and Mustardseed; or, as we might say, penicillin. Sweet Puck, who administers the purple juice, is thus truly the spirit of this play, as his nicknames enact its tactics of appeasement. By literally reducing him to a diminutive, *A Midsummer Night's Dream* placates the Evil Eye with the most apotropaic of devices, euphemism: a figure, as Goethe defined it, 'by which we reject what we fear,' not by expulsion but

[47] Thomas, op. cit. (note 44), pp. 728 and 30–1.
[48] C. Ginzburg, *The Night Battles: Witchcraft and Agrarian Cults in the Sixteenth and Seventeenth Centuries*, trans. J. and A. Tedeschi (London, 1983).

by circumlocution.[49] And since two of his kinder names are Hermes and Mercury, it is apt that Robin is the messenger of a plot that depends, as Quince says, on such 'translation' (III, i, 112). For what is lost in translation by Shakespeare's metamorphosis of Ovid is the Bacchic violence of both myth and history. So, where Collingbourne had been 'hanged, cut down, and had his bowels ripped out of his belly and cast into the fire,'[50] this author adopts a mask of meek 'simplicity,' like Quince, to pay his 'poor duty' (V, i, 91) to 'They that have power to hurt and will do none' (*Sonnet 94*) if properly addressed:

> *Approach, ye Furies fell!*
> *O Fates, come, come!*
> *Cut thread and thrum:*
> *Quail, crush, conclude, and quell.*   (V, i, 273–6)

Bottom had promised to 'tear a passion to tatters' as Hercules (*Hamlet*, III, ii, 10), and now his histrionics remind us that one Herculean feat had been to rescue Theseus from Hades by making the Furies drunk.[51] So, if Hecate and the Erinnyes figure England's Queen and court in the eyes of Shakespeare's players, Quince's bombast seems an epitome of that self-irony which functions, according to Pierre Bourdieu, with every linguistic offering, but never more abjectly than in the anxiety of the *petit bourgeois* towards their products, 'which pushes them into paroxysms on formal occasions, or rash utterances of artificial confidence.'[52] Theseus observes just such 'hyper-correction' when clerks 'shiver and look pale, / Make periods in the midst of sentences' and 'Throttle their practis'd accent in their fears'; and he knows it is through this 'modesty of fearful duty' that his own power is 'misrecognised' (in Bourdieu's terms) as an anodyne 'symbolic violence' (V, i, 93–101). These Athenians already grasp the post-structuralist theory that censorship is best exercised as 'euphemization

---

[49] Quoted in K. Burke, *The Philosophy of Literary Form: Studies in Symbolic Action* (rev. ed. New York, 1957), p. 46. For euphemism, see also M.K. Adler, *Naming and Addressing* (London, 1978), pp. 53–4, 78–81, 100; and F.T. Elworthy, *The Evil Eye: An Account of this Ancient Superstition* (repr. New York, 1989), passim.
[50] R. Fabyan, *The New Chronicles of England and France*, ed. H. Ellis (London, 1811), p. 672, quoted in V.J. Scattergood, *Politics and Poetry in the Fifteenth Century* (London, 1971), p. 21.
[51] R. Graves, *The Greek Myths* (Harmondsworth, 1955), Vol. 1, pp. 224–5.
[52] P. Bourdieu, *Language and Symbolic Power*, trans. G. Raymond & M. Adamson (London, 1992), pp. 82–3.

imposed on producers of symbolic goods . . . which condemns the dominated either to silence or shocking outspokenness.' For by reducing the Angry Ones to mirth, the mechanicals allow them 'to take what they mistake' (90), and so invoke 'the gentle, unrecognised violence of debts and gifts.' Overt censorship was never as complete, since now 'the agent is censored once and for all.'[53]

'Behold her silver visage in the watery glass' (I, i, 112): despite the danger of divining with mirror and moon, Shakespeare at last reveals the image of his Queen. Pyramus's call to the 'Sisters Three' identifies the Ladies before whom the action has been played (V, i, 323); and Amazons, Maenads, and Queens are all implicated in the verdict of these Fates and Furies by the sentences they too pass on the artisan, artist, and art. For Ginzburg's *benandanti*, the night judges were the 'wild hunt' of witches, who were pacified with oblations, like those left in Shakespeare's city, of food and drink; and for Frazer's Greeks, they were souls of the dead, to be appeased with a mock marriage and murder, like Bottom's, of a man in animal skin.[54] As Girard remarks, Shakespeare is a comparativist in anthropology,[55] and what he compares are ancient and modern rites to propitiate the powers that be. So, though the Epilogue frets whether the actors will 'have unearned luck . . . to 'scape the serpent's tongue' that menaced Hermia (419–20), these Furies are soon defanged, for are they not indeed the Eumenides, whose name – The Kindly Ones – was given them in Athens? Hippolyta speaks for them all when she admits, 'I pity the man' (279), and Medusa's face dissolves in smiles. With such sweet sorrow royalty secures consent, for its frightening Ladies are all 'good fellows' when the *Dream* forgets the violence that it dreamt. So, unlike Orpheus, whose song 'drew savage beasts,' but was ended by '*Bacchus* drunken rout' when 'they murdered him, that never till that hour did utter words in vain,'[56] this author will be applauded when his Lion brings forth sweetness to turn death into a figure of speech: 'And

[53] Ibid., pp. 137–8; P. Bourdieu, *The Logic of Practice*, trans. R. Nice (Cambridge, 1990), p. 127.
[54] Ginzburg, op. cit. (note 48), pp. 22–5 (and for the folk motif of the 'wild hunt' of the wandering dead, see pp. 42–50); J. Frazer, *The Golden Bough: V: Spirits of the Corn and of the Wild* (London, 1912), p. 30. For the English custom of leaving out food and drink, such as Puck 'skims', as a night-time offering to Fairies (or the dead), see Thomas, op. cit. (note 44), p. 728.
[55] Girard, op. cit. (note 11), p. 237.
[56] Ovid, op. cit. (note 16), XI, 18, 41–2. In Golding Apollo 'Dispoints the Serpent of his bit' when it is about to feed on Orpheus's disembodied head (65).

the Duke had not given him sixpence a day for playing . . . I'll be hang'd' (IV, ii, 21). The fable he 'preferred' (37) prompted his tact, being spun out in Ovid to cheat the Bacchae of prey; but Shakespeare knew better than his idol, who died exiled by Augustus for indiscretion, the importance of deflecting tragedy with 'sport':

> If we shadows have offended,
> Think but this, and all is mended,
> That you have but slumbered here,
> While these visions did appear.
> And this weak and idle theme,
> No more yielding but a dream.   (V, i, 409–14)

'Fairies away!' (II, i, 144): by collapsing his own meaning into the diminutiveness of an inaccessible aesthetic domain, this poet tamed the Furies into Fairies where Orpheus and Ovid failed, and ensured his troupe became 'but shadows' of reality (208), and not shades. As Marx appreciated, Shakespeare's dreaming played its part in the containment of civic violence which determined that, though London suffered all the overpopulation, unemployment, inflation, and plague endemic in early modern cities, it did not experience the chronic conflict that raged elsewhere. The nightmare of the Tudor regime – that the weaver of Southwark would make cause with the 'heavy ploughman' of Kent (V, i, 359), incited by some 'pale companion' of the elite – was prevented by a rapprochement Shakespeare symbolised in his multiple converging plot; whilst the Crown learned from the rioting of 1595 that the secret of stability was, as he envisaged, satisfaction of London's appetite for 'good hay, sweet hay' (IV, i, 33) through regular supply of corn. History suggests that the thing of greatest constancy that grew on Bankside from the story of the citizens' mad Midsummer night, was a network of 'barns and garners never empty' (The Tempest, IV, i, 111), 'for laying up of wheat and service of the city,' together with 'certain Ovens purposely made to bake out the bread corn of the said garners, for relief of the poor citizens, when need should require.'[57] It was by such management that the paradoxical outcome of the famine of the 1590s was, as A Midsummer

---

[57] J. Stow, 'Borough of Southwark', in A Survey of London (London, 1603; repr. Oxford, 1908), ed. C.L. Kingsford, p. 65. For London's surprising stability in the early modern period, see also S. Rappaport, 'Social Structure and Mobility in Sixteenth Century London', 2 parts, in The London Journal, 9: 2 (Winter 1983), pp. 107–35; and 10: 2 (Winter 1984), pp. 107–34.

Night's Dream had foreseen, not the overthrow but the strengthening of municipal order, since, though Shakespeare's England 'was not capable of eliminating dearth, it was capable of interpreting the phenomenon to preserve itself. Society emerged from the crisis with its values and authority reinforced, for dearth highlighted the one and enhanced the other.'[58]

It had been Orpheus and his surrogates, according to Ovid and Frazer, who were ploughed into the ground to restore the crops;[59] and in the Greece of the *Dream* the death of the author serves an equivalent symbolic effacement: 'No epilogue, I pray you; for your play needs no excuse . . . when the players are all dead, there need none to be blamed' (V, i, 341–3). Bottom's ballad to 'expound' the story of the night will never now be told; for, given rope to hang himself, its author submits instead to an aesthetic closure. Yet, 'How he terrifies me,' wrote Rilke of Shakespeare's actual Epilogues, 'This man who draws the wire into his head, and hangs himself / Beside the other puppets, and henceforth / Begs mercy of the play.'[60] Theseus speaks for English monarchy, when he comments on such self-erasure: 'The kinder we, to give them thanks for nothing' (89). The Kindly Ones knew the Bard's 'tongue-tied' silence constituted their 'welcome' (100–5), and they rewarded him with the preferment of which he dreamt. The poet returned the kindness, avoiding, even when saluting their Garter investiture, or when the Queen died, writing his sovereign's or her successor's name.[61] Thus, England's Ovid kept faith with what Frazer calls a 'debt to the savage': the taboo hedging kings with divinity by punishing mention of them, and even causing their names to be thrown on tablets into the sea.[62] No wonder the dynasty

---

58 J. Walter and K. Wrightson, 'Dearth and the Social Order in Early Modern England', in *Past and Present*, 71 (May 1976), p. 42.
59 Ovid, op. cit. (note 16), XI, 53; Frazer, op. cit. (note 50), pp. 16–34; *The Golden Bough: IV: Adonis, Attis, Osiris: Studies in the History of Oriental Religion* (London, 1907), pp. 330–4.
60 R.M. Rilke, 'The Spirit Ariel', in *Selected Poems of Rainer Maria Rilke*, trans. J.B. Leishmann (Harmondsworth, 1964), p. 74.
61 Henry Chettle chided Shakespeare in *England's Mourning Garment* (1603) for failing to 'Drop from his honey-tongued muse one sable tear / To mourn her death that grac'd his deserts, / And to his lays opened her royal ear. / Shepherd, remember our Elizabeth'; but Shakespeare, as Chambers says, 'was not drawn' (*Sources for a Biography of Shakespeare* (Oxford, 1946), p. 49). The one occasion when he did name Queen Elizabeth was at her christening in *Henry VIII* (V, v, 1–9); but he never referred to King James by name at all.
62 Frazer, op. cit. (note 50), pp. 357–9.

shook his hand when he promised to 'restore amends' and weave a
vapid 'nothing' about their names and habitations (V, i, 424). So
while the London 'lion roars' and the Irish 'wolf behowls the moon,'
his Fairies' last treat will be to bless the 'palace with sweet peace' to
ensure the 'owner of it blest, / Ever shall in safety rest' (V, i, 403–6).
Thus, by euphemising its absent present, Shakespeare's mirror of allusion repelled its history back with a curse of 'Evil to him who evil
thinks.' For it was this royal motto which gave the author a poetics of
circumspection to turn the Evil Eye upon itself:

> To Windsor chimneys shalt thou leap,
> Where fires thou findest unrack'd and hearths unswept . . .
> Search Windsor Castle, elves, within and out,
> Strew good luck, ouphes, on every sacred room,
> That it may stand till the perpetual doom . . .
> And *Honi soit qui mal y pense* write
> In emerald tufts, flowers purple, blue and white.
> (*The Merry Wives of Windsor*, V, v, 43–70)

'Backed by our supreme authority, / He'll command a large ma-
jority': the endorsement of Britain's leadership by W.S. Gilbert's
Queen of the Fairies expressed a fundamental truth about the
Shakespearean constitution Marx described.[63] And for generations
Shakespeare's 'fairy charactery' (73) did guard the House at Windsor,
until in another horrible year of another *fin-de-siècle* we were at last
reminded that neither play nor palace can escape the 'drowsy fire' of
history that smoulders where 'the wasted brands do glow' (V, i, 361–
78), when 'Everything happened in a few moments, as if for centuries
those ancient pages had been yearning for arson and were rejoicing in
the sudden satisfaction of their desire' for flame.[64]

---

63 W.S. Gilbert, *Iolanthe* (1882), Act 3.
64 U. Eco, *The Name of the Rose*, trans. W. Weaver (London, 1983), p. 483.

The Shattered Violl: *print and textuality in the 1640s*

LUCASTA MILLER

AREOPAGITICA, MILTON'S FAMOUS PLEA for the 'liberty of unlicenc'd printing', posits an ideal relationship between authors and texts: books 'preserve as in a violl the purest efficacie and extraction of that living intellect that bred them.'[1] The simile suggests that the author's intention is unproblematically immanent within the text. As a phial, the text acts as a protective capsule, insulating its contents from dissipation or decay. And if, by implication, it is a glass phial, it also offers transparent access to the author's 'intellect' inside. As a self-contained unit, the phial/text floats free of the need to anchor itself in the external authority represented by the licenser. Validated solely by the presence of the author within it, the ideal text is independent and authenticates itself.

Abbe Blum has argued that *Areopagitica's* central contradiction stems from the fact that it promotes the autonomy of the author from public institutions, but that by doing so in the public medium of print it remains bound up in the power relations it seeks to escape.She suggests that Milton cannot separate the notion of authorial independence from the idea of threats to that independence.[2] Rather than concentrating on the threats offered by censorship to the author, this article will attempt to show how the *absence* of effective censorship controls in the early 1640s – when the centre of censoring power was shifting from the crown to Parliament and agencies like the Stationers' Company were left in limbo regarding the source of their authority – provoked an ambivalent response.[3] If this lapse helped to

1 *The Complete Prose Works of John Milton*, ed. Don M. Wolfe et al., 8 vols. (Yale, 1953ff), II. 492. All subsequent page references to prose works by Milton refer to this volume.
2 Abbe Blum, 'The Author's Authority *Areopagitica* and the Labour of Licensing', in *Remembering Milton: Essays on the texts and traditions*, ed. Mary Nyquist and Margaret W. Ferguson (London, 1988), 74–96.
3 For a more detailed historical account see F.S. Siebert, *Freedom of the Press in England 1476–1776* (Urbana, Ill., 1952), ch. 8, 'Chaos in the Printing Trade'.

fuel the proliferation of controversialist texts in print, the apparent anarchy of the pamphlet war – described by contemporaries as a latter-day Babel – served to undermine the ideal conception of textuality contained in Milton's image of the 'violl'.[4] Recent developments in bibliographical criticism have heralded a move, in D.F. McKenzie's words, away from 'questions of authorial intention and textual authority to those of textual dissemination and readership'.[5] Focussing on Milton's divorce tracts and their reception, this article will explore Mackenzie's dichotomy within the seventeenth-century context, by exploring a series of moments at which these texts reveal self-consciousness or anxiety as to their own textuality or printed status. The ideal conception of texts as authoritative authorial containers can be seen to coexist uneasily with the awareness of a printed text's instability as it circulates promiscuously in the marketplace.

The centrality of Scripture in seventeenth-century discourse and the concordant rhetoric of the 'book of nature' suggest a notion of 'text' associated with divine order. The concept of the authoritative text is central to the divorce tracts' exegetical mode of argument. Even when they allude to supposedly 'non-textual' methods of argument 'from reason', the imagery employed indicates the importance of the idea of 'text' as an authenticating force. Thus, *a priori* argument reveals natural laws 'charactered' on the human heart. And, in *Tetrachordon*, reason itself becomes synonymous with text, where Milton appeals to 'those whose reason is not an illiterate booke to themselves' (p. 636). By transferring the epithet 'illiterate' from reader to text, Milton implies a textuality which writes out the reader, just as the ideal Scripture text is capable of 'explaining itself' independent of an exegete. This reflects *Areopagitica's* 'violl' image, which appears to locate the meaning of a text in the mind of the author rather than in reader response. Authoritative textuality depends on suppressing the ideas of readership and dissemination. But any awareness of the experience of putting a printed text into circulation serves to undermine the stability associated with the ideal notion of textuality.

Milton may have expressed the hope that time, the midwife of truth, would declare his heterodox divorce doctrine legitimate. But

---

[4] For a discussion of the pamphlet war as Babel see Sharon Achinstein, 'The Politics of Babel' in *Pamphlet Wars: Prose in the English Revolution*, ed. James Holstun (London, 1992), 14–44.
[5] Quoted in review article by Warwick Gould, 'Strategies for Hermeneuts', *TLS* 26 June 1992, p. 23.

during the five years after the initial publication of *The Doctrine and Discipline of Divorce* in 1643, the result of its dissemination was its repeated bastardisation in print. In 1644, the first hostile printed allusions – made by William Prynne and Herbert Palmer – attempted to identify it with the sectaries.[6] It received only one full-length refutation in print – the anonymous *An Answer to a Book, Intituled, The Doctrine and Discipline of Divorce* – and the other allusions which followed reflected the pattern set by Prynne and Palmer, conflating Milton's text with a range of other supposed subversive beliefs and practices in the interests of anti-sectarian propaganda. Milton's divorce doctrine was anthologised in the heresy catalogues of Robert Baillie, Ephraim Pagitt, and Thomas Edwards.[7] And by 1647 it was deemed suitable for inclusion in (among others) a sensationalist scandal-sheet, *A Catalogue of the Severall Sects and Opinions in England and Other Nations*. Here, the complexities of Milton's divorce argument are reduced to the non-verbal level of a crude pictorial representation of a 'Divorcer' beating his wife. Milton had unwittingly generated a mythical sect. In the unregulated marketplace of the pamphlet war, his texts on divorce had broken free from authorial control, revealing themselves to be vulnerable to appropriation, deconstruction, and reconstruction by rival texts, and to be capable of generating unintended fictions. Thomas Edwards's *Gangraena* defined *The Doctrine and Discipline of Divorce* as a sectarian text not by appealing to its author's intentions but by reference to its supposed readership, alleging its influence on the radical Mrs Attaway.[8] In dissemination, a text could no longer function as an ideally autonomous container preserving its author's 'living intellect'. Participating in a socially generated matrix of textual practices, the printed text could reveal itself as radically unstable.

---

6   William Prynne, *Twelve Considerable Serious Questions touching Church Government* (London, 1644); Herbert Palmer, *The Glasse of Gods Providence towards His Faithfull Ones. Held forth in a Sermon preached to the two Houses of Parliament, at Margarets Westminster, Aug. 13 1644* (London, 1644).
7   Robert Baillie, *A Dissuasive from the Errours of the Time: Wherein the Tenets of the principall Sects, especially of the Independents, are drawn together in one Map, for the most part, in the words of their own Authors* (London, 1645); Ephraim Pagitt, *Heresiography: or A description of the Hereticks and Sectaries of these latter times* (London, 1645); Thomas Edwards, *Gangraena: or a Catalogue and Discovery of many of the Errours, Heresies, Blasphemies and pernicious Practices of the Sectaries of this time* (London, 1646), 3 parts.
8   Thomas Edwards, *Gangraena: the Second Part* (London, 1646), pp. 10–11.

Ironically, *Areopagitica's* image of the 'violl' already contains covert fears as to the author's ability to control the text's production of meanings. The spelling suggests a musical pun. This may of course connote a harmonious relationship between author and text. But, more ambiguously, a viol is a *hollow* instrument, unlike the phial which is filled with its intellectual contents. The viol's ability to give voice is dependent on its player; perhaps a text's ability to make meanings is dependent on its readers. The fear that the author may not be able to control the meaning of his text is also present in the imagery of birth – a frequent Miltonic metaphor for textual creativity – in 'the living intellect that bred them'. It places the author in a parental role. But *Tetrachordon* cites the lawfulness of a child's autonomy in choosing a marriage partner 'without the Fathers consent' (pp. 604–05). Once the textual brainchild is circulating in the promiscuous world of the marketplace, there is the anxiety that it might indeed spring up an armed man, capable, if reconstructed by hostile critics, of parricide.

If Milton's metaphors suggest anxieties that intentionality might not, after all, be immanent in the text, his overtly stated hermeneutic promotes the recovery of authorial intention as the touchstone of right reading. The humanist exegetical method pursued in the divorce tracts historicises the sacred text. And Milton's interpretation, for example, of Christ's confrontation with the Pharisees brings the criteria of stylistic decorum to bear with the object of reconstructing Christ's 'intention' in specific local circumstances (p. 283).

Yet, while identifying the exegete's aim as the recovery of divine intention, Milton reveals this aim to be problematic. The identity of the Bible's authorial subject becomes slippery. Whereas *The Doctrine and Discipline of Divorce's* prefatory address attributes the Pentateuch to Moses (not God), Christ, and not the Evangelists, is the author of the Gospels. Elsewhere, Moses, or the other prophets, are characterised not as authors but as amanuenses to God. And if the author's identity is unstable, the rhetoric used to describe the restoration of intention is similarly shifty, revealing latent doubts:

> From which words so plain, lesse cannot be concluded, nor is by any learned Interpreter, then that in God's intention [marriage is] a meet and happy conversation. (p. 246)

The passive construction suggests an active attempt to suppress the exegete's – potentially distorting – role as reader. The double negative injects doubt into the positive assertion. And the indefinite reference to 'any learned interpreter' functions as a rhetorical shield rather than a genuine argument 'from authority'. Milton's defensive rhetoric undermines his assertion of the unproblematic accessibility of the author's intention.

Milton's fears concerning the text's ability to act as an ideal transparent authorial container are connected with anxieties about the nature of actual printed textuality. When he attempts to assert the immanence of the divine intention in the text of the Bible he uses a metaphor which implicitly casts doubt on the capacity of graphic or typographic discourse to represent intention. He rejects one particular reading of a textual crux because:

it introduces in a new manner the person of God speaking less Majestic than he is ever wont; When God speaks by his Profet he ever speaks in the first person; thereby signifying his Majesty and omni-presence. (p. 616)

To represent God speaking in the third person would be 'to shrink [his] glorious omnipresence . . . into a kind of circumscriptive absence' and would 'absent the person of God from his own words as if he came not along with them' (p. 616). Suggesting that the presence of the author's 'person' is essential if his words are to retain their full intentional value, Milton transforms the written text into an oral fiction (God is represented as 'speaking'). In contrast to the presence of the speaker in the spoken, writing is associated with absence. 'Circumscriptive absence', with its writerly connotations, even stresses the visual nature of graphic discourse by literally describing the circular appearance of a cipher on the page. The written text is, by implication, alienated from its author: the speaker's bodily presence is necessary if his words are to remain authentic.

Milton's use of metaphors of speech and presence suggest anxieties as to the ability of the printed text to convey intention. Speech, rather than writing or print, becomes the paradigm for authentic language use. The continuing primacy of oral discourse in early modern culture has been described by Keith Thomas:

Oral communication remained central, whether as speeches in Parliament, pleadings in the law courts, teaching in the schools, or preaching and catechising in church. Despite their reliance on the

Bible and Prayer Book, the clergy still expected their flock to learn articles of belief by heart and to listen to spoken sermons.[9]

And, if speech remained central within the context of linguistic practice, it is also fundamental for the theorists of the 1650s, John Wallis and Meric Casaubon, who attempt to connect the ability of language to carry meaning with the oral process of vocalisation. Wallis's *Grammatica Lingua Anglicanae* (1653) seeks the elusive connection between words and things in onomatopoeic correspondences. Casaubon, discussing 'Rhetoricall Enthusiasme' (in *A Treatise concerning Enthusiasme*, 2nd edn. 1656), takes speech, rather than writing as his paradigm for language, giving a detailed description of 'the inward fabric of the mouth, by which words, with aire, are formed' (p. 181), and asserting that the communicative efficacy of words stems from their 'rhythmos' or phonic dimension, which has a 'natural property or influence upon the soul of man' (p. 236). In *Leviathan*, Hobbes prioritises oral discourse, giving the title of his section on language theory as 'Of Speech', and placing speech at the top of his hierarchy of human linguistic achievement, with writing next, and printing – 'no great matter' – at the bottom.

An analysis of the cross-section of 1640s pamphlets represented by the divorce tracts and the matrix of contemporary texts alluding to them reveals a self-conscious awareness of the tensions between oral and typographic discourse. John Wilkins's *Ecclesiastes, Or, A Discourse concerning the Gift of Preaching as it fals under the rules of Art* (1647) confidently attempts to displace speech into print by describing its rules for structuring an oral sermon in a visual, tabulated form which exploits the typography of Ramist-style brackets. But Daniel Featley's *The Dippers dipt* and Herbert Palmer's *The Glasse of God's Providence*, both of which advertise themselves as transcripts of oral performances, express anxieties about the adequacy of the printed word.[10]

Palmer's attitude towards printed textuality is radically ambiguous. Using print as a metaphor for the divine order inscribed in the natural law of social hierarchy, he appeals to an ideal notion of the world as text:

---

[9] K.V. Thomas, 'The Meaning of Literacy in Early Modern England' in Gerd Baumann, ed. *The Written Word: Literacy in Transition* (Oxford, 1986).
[10] Daniel Featley, *The Dippers dipt, Or, the Anabaptists duck'd and plunged Over Head and Eares, at a Disputation in Southwark* (London, 1645); Herbert Palmer, *The Glasse of God's Providence* (1644).

> the Ground of Humane Authority, is that GOD is pleased to print some
> characters of the Image of his Majestie in the faces of Superiours, and
> stamp the counter-part of it upon the hearts of the Inferiours. (p. 54)

Yet the experience of transforming his oral sermon into an actual
printed text conflicts with this apparent faith in printed textuality. No
longer symbolic of God's order, it becomes a dubious channel through
which to communicate his Word, and no substitute for the authenticity of speech:

> And though Faith most commonly comes by Hearing, yet unques-
> tionable Experience telling us, that it is partly encreased by Reading
> also, (specially of what was once attentively heard). (unpaginated
> preface)

The divine unity of 'that Word which divers weeks ago [God] sent to
be preached in your ears' is collapsed into the fragmentary, uncapi-
talised 'these words' which are now to appear on the printed page.
Palmer exhibits self-conscious awareness of the different bodily experiences of oral and printed communication, the one involving the
'ears', the other the 'hands and eyes'. And the fact that he addresses
his readership in the second person, assuming it will consist of the
same parliamentary audience which heard his spoken sermon, suggests
a desire to suppress the fact that the circulation of a printed text is
potentially arbitrary. Whereas oral preaching necessarily involves the
combined physical presence of orator and audience, the author of a
printed text is absent, dislocated and unable to see or control his
readership. Ultimately, Palmer's anxieties about entering into printed
debate are paralleled in his fears that the divinely printed text of
natural law is itself in the process of being destabilised. God as printer
threatens to unbalance his own handiwork:

> And if it please GOD . . . to blot out that stamp which was upon
> Inferiours hearts, they presently withdraw all respect from such
> Superiours. (p. 54)

Printing his sermon will inevitably involve Palmer in the controversial discourse of the pamphlet war, a discourse which is symbolic of
civil disintegration. And fears as to the instability of actual printed
textuality, highlighted during the period of the pamphlet war, spill
over into the realm of the ideal notion of the world as a divine text
through which God reveals his intentions.

Like Palmer, Daniel Featley expresses doubts as to the efficacy of print in comparison to speech. Exhibiting a similar self-conscious awareness of the different bodily experiences of writing and speaking, the preface to *The Dippers dipt* suggests the superiority of oral discourse:

> And preach the Gospel I can no otherwise, for both my pulpits are taken from me. Now therefore since I cannot lingua, I must be content as I am able to evangelizare calumo, to preach with my pen. (sig. C1r)

A Royalist removed from his living, Featley may be using 'pulpits' as a metonymy for the loss of social position, property, income, and authority he has incurred. But the specific references to 'tongue' and 'pen' suggest that its function is more literal, exposing an awareness of the physical presence of the preacher in contrast to the writer's absence.

The main body of *The Dippers dipt* purports to be 'a true relation of the meeting in Southwark between Dr Daniel Featley and a company of Anabaptists', which had taken place on 17 October 1642. As a printed transcript of an oral event, it explores the interface between the two forms of discourse. But though Featley's preface suggests the inadequacy of graphic communication, the 'true relation' actively exploits its printed status, using the material semantics of typography to counteract the bodily absence of the disputants and to give Featley the strategic advantage. Cast in the form of a dialogue, the 'true relation' presents Featley's speeches in roman type, while the Anabaptists' contributions are printed in italics. The opposition between self and outlandish other, which informs the discourse of anti-sectarian propaganda, becomes visible on the page – the individual, unnamed Anabaptists are typographically amalgamated into a single Other. Roman type is also used for any 'neutral' narrative passages outside the dialogue. This implicitly presents Featley's opinions as objective, by visually identifying him with the voice of an impersonal omniscient narrator. Featley's overall strategy is to assert his own learning (his use of Latin tags is typical) and reveal the inadequacy of his opponents', in an attempt to expose their demands for independence from the established church as invalid in the light of their inability to perform the priestly office of 'teacher'. 'If you will dispute by reason,' he tells the Anabaptists, 'you must conclude syllogistically . . . which I take to be out of your element' (p. 2). Ironically, Featley's dialectical mode of argument relies heavily on the special typographic arrangement of syllogisms which contrives to give his logic an authoritative appearance unavailable in oral performance.

If *The Dippers dipt* attempts to exploit its printed status, the divorce tracts reveal a less confident response to the authorial absence engendered by print. Milton reacts to this disembodiment by constructing fictional oratorical scenarios, in the addresses to Parliament which preface three of the divorce tracts and in *Areopagitica*. These addresses make use of a fictional first person authorial presence:

> Nor have I whether to appeal, but to the concourse of so much piety and wisdom heer assembl'd. Bringing in my hands an ancient statute of Moses. (p. 224)

Orator and audience are brought together into the same locality ('heer'), and the speaker's bodily presence is dramatised ('hands'). Yet anxieties concerning the alienated relationship between author and readership are exposed where Milton expresses frustration at being unable to 'see' his opponents:

> Yet that the author may be known to ground himself upon his own innocence, and the merit of his cause, not upon the favour of a diversion, or a delay in any just censure, but wishes rather he might see those his detracters at any fair meeting . . . I shall here briefly single one of them. (p. 579)

The grammatical anacoluthon whereby Milton employs both first and third person self-references in the same sentence suggests discomfort in the process of re-presenting the self in the disembodied medium of print. In the context of Milton's analysis of 'God speaking' discussed above, the use of the third person 'absents' the author. And the absence of the author could, in the context of printed political conflict, become a threat. Not only does it leave the text open to hostile reconstruction. It also permits the possibility of forgery, exemplified in Edward Hyde's *Two Speeches Made in the House of Peers* (1643), which purports to be a transcript of oral performances by Lord Brooke and Lord Pembroke. Hyde's text was taken for genuine by its readers, and Lord Brooke complained of being 'much reproached for so unChristian a speech'.[11]

---

[11] Cited in Ernest Sirluck's Introduction, *The Complete Prose Works of John Milton*, II. 57.

Lord Brooke's complaint introduces the question of dissemination: an author – even an alleged author – is vulnerable to hostile reconstruction at the hands of his readership. The appropriation of *The Doctrine and Discipline of Divorce* by anti-sectarian propagandists can be related to the failure of the first edition to employ strategies designed to target and manipulate their readers. And the second edition displays an increased awareness of readership. Analogous texts of the period reveal attempts to assert their authorised status and regulate reader response, whereas the first divorce tract initially came out unlicensed, anonymous, and without a preface. In contrast, the English translation of Bernardino Ochino's heterodox *A Dialogue of Polygamy*, which was published together with *A Dialogue of Divorce* in 1656, attempts to sanitise its controversial subject matter by displaying the licenser's imprimatur and describing its author's Protestant credentials. It also contains an introductory epistle from 'the Stationer to the Reader', characterising 'the Discourse it self' as nonpolemical – 'it asserts nothing, positively determines nothing' – and asserting that 'no discreet person (whatever he thinks of the point) should find himself offended' (sig. A4v). It deflects criticism by overtly attempting to instil in the reader the moral imperative to 'read this Treatise soberly' (sig. A5v). If the Stationer takes the protective measure of interposing himself between the author of the dialogue and its reader in order to secure a non-hostile response, John Selden's *Uxor Ebraica* (1646) places a limit on its potential readership. Like Milton's tract, it investigates Old Testament marital mores. But, taking an antiquarian rather than polemical stance, it does so in Latin, thus excluding 'outlandish' readers like the infamous Mrs Attaway, who had allegedly read and been influenced by Milton's text.

Alluding to the problem of regulating readership, the second edition of *The Doctrine and Discipline of Divorce* concedes that 'it might perhaps more fitly have been written in another tongue'. *Tetrachordon*'s Greek title and title-page quotation from Euripides function as an assertion of their author's humanist civility in contrast to the social inferiority of the sectarian stereotype from which Milton is at pains to dissociate himself. But as well as helping to project an authoritative image of the author, these elements of the title page implicitly function as an attempt to target a suitable readership. Where the first edition of *The Doctrine and Discipline of Divorce* contains no awareness of its imaginary audience, and does not identify its author, the second edition attempts to flesh out these absences. Without them, Milton's text has been vulnerable to hostile reconstruction. In the second edition he reveals his own identity and adds a direct address to 'the Parliament of England with the Assembly'. And the addition of an apostrophe to Parliament at the end of the text indicates that not only the prefatory address but the whole body of the text has been reconceived along the lines of reader response.

Changes in the second edition also suggest a desire to improve the tract's readability. Where the first edition is a piece of continuous prose, the second is divided into two books and subdivided into chapters with headings. This awareness of readership is paralleled in the additions which imply a heightened rhetorical consciousness. The interpolation of the fable of Eros and Anteros represents an attempt to fulfil the orator's aim of persuading his audience, reflecting the advice given in Thomas Wilson's standard rhetorical handbook: 'The feigned fables . . . not only . . . delite the rude and ignorant, but also they helpe much for persuasion [for] such as speak in open audience.'[12] Wilson refers to spoken (as opposed to printed) oratory, and Milton's addition of the fable could also be seen to function as a metaphorical attempt to counteract the disembodiment of print by concretising an abstract argument. Yet the author's absence from the printed text – and the impossibility of a 'fair meeting' between the disputants in a printed debate – continue to arouse anxieties.

Colasterion, Milton's attack on the *Answer to a Book, Intituled, The Doctrine and Discipline of Divorce*, exposes such anxieties. Though its title – meaning 'place of punishment' – exploits the fictional co-presence of the disputants in a specific locality, the anonymity of the Answerer (in which the disembodiment of print colludes) leads to inconsistencies in Milton's mode of addressing his critic. Shifting between the third and second persons – 'His first Argument. . . . Your second Argument' (p. 730) – he reveals doubts as to whether a direct attack is possible in the medium of print. Despite the fact that he claims to have discovered that the *Answer* is a collaborative effort, he prefers to refer to a singular Answerer in the third person. The Smectymnuans resolved their multiple authorship into one name, and, of all the texts in the allusive matrix surrounding the divorce tracts, those of known multiple authorship suppress this fact on their title pages.[13] More than one author might suggest the fragmentation of

---

[12] Thomas Wilson, *The arte of Rhetorique* (1560), ed. G.H. Mair (Oxford, 1909), pp. 197–8.
[13] For example, *Hell Broke Loose*, an official parliamentary publication

intentionality, deprivatising it and undermining the ideal unity of text and author.

Milton reacts to the indeterminate identity of the absent Answerer, engendered by the dislocated relationship between author and printed text, by employing metaphorical 'embodying' strategies. Thomas N. Corns has described *Colasterion* as a 'quest for respectability' in which Milton employs the methods of the anti-sectarian propagandist to distance himself from the sects with whom he has been identified.[14] Similarities between Daniel Featley's rhetoric and *Colasterion*'s reinforce Corns's argument. Featley's use of the motif of inferior social rank in the construction of a sectarian stereotype is paralleled in Milton's attacks on the Answerer as a 'servingman . . . turned sollicitor'. Both use puns which deflate elite theological activity into the physical labour of the lower orders. Featley describes the world turned upside down in a series of tropes: 'I am to tell thee of new changes...stables into temples . . . shopboards into communion tables . . . cooks instead of mincing the meat fall upon dividing the word' (sig. C2r). And Milton uses a similar punning device to attack the Answerer:

> Now he comes to the Position, which I sett down whole; and like an able text man slits it into fowr, that hee may the better come at it with his Barbar Surgery, and his sleevs turn'd up. (p. 736–7)

In the polemical context, Milton is undermining the Answerer's credibility by exposing his supposed inferior social status. In the context of anxieties concerning printed textuality, his attempts to dramatise the Answerer performing a range of menial domestic tasks are motivated by the desire to give body to the absent author.

The prologue to Milton's punishment of the Answerer deals similarly with other offenders, including Prynne, whose *Twelve Considerable Serious Questions* had alluded unfavourably to the divorce tract. Here, Milton describes the moment at which he received Prynne's pamphlet, constructing a bodily presence for himself: 'it was my hap

which was written by committee, suppresses the identities of its authors (given in the *Commons Journal*, 27 January 1646/7) as discrete individuals, resolving their multiplicity into the singularity of the parliamentary clerk who is named.

[14] Thomas N. Corns, 'Milton's Quest for Respectability', *MLR*, 77 (1982), pp. 769–79.

. . . lighting upon a certain parcel of *Quaeries* . . . I stood awhile and wonder'd . . . But as I still was waiting . . . a book was brought to my hands' (p. 722–4). Ironically, the fact that he stresses the physical presence of the 'book' serves to compound, not dispel, the dislocation between author and text. *Areopagtica*'s alchemical fiction of the ideal text as a phial containing the author's intellectual essence defines books as created from spiritual substance and suppresses their material aspect. But the intrusion of an awareness of texts as physical objects undermines the ideal, since the author is alienated from a text's mechanical production in the print shop, and the fact that the printed artifact is the result of collaborative labour potentially fragments the unity of authorial intention. Milton's attempts to construct a bodily presence for his critics are ironically focused on the organ of speech – Prynne, for example, has yeilded 'his mouth to bee the common road of Truth and Falshood' (p. 723). But the repeated use of the isolated image of the mouth undermines the attempt at counteracting the disembodiment of print; in fact it reveals bodily absence.

Colasterion's attitudes towards textuality are fundamentally conflicting. On the one hand it portrays the text as a glass in which not only the author's intention, but his whole personality, are unproblematically visible: Milton infers the Answerer's 'character' from the 'flat and rude' nature of his 'stile' (p. 725), and thence constructs a persona to fill the authorial absence of the printed text. In doing so, he employs the convention of Renaissance rhetorical theory outlined in Puttenham's *Arte of English Poesie*, which describes 'stile' as 'the image of mind (mentis character)'.[15] Yet the printing connotations of 'character' (literally suggesting the idea of 'imprint') become ambiguous in the context of the insecurities Milton elsewhere reveals as to the authenticity of printed discourse. And Milton's attempt to construct a stable presence for the Answerer is ironically undermined by the methods he uses to deconstruct the *Answer*. Revealing his opponent's text to generate meanings which completely contradict its overtly stated intention – *Colasterion* even italicises Milton's parodies of the *Answer*, duplicitously parading them as quotations – he enacts a denial of the stable presence of authorial intention. The reader usurps the office of making meanings.

If the early 1640s saw a proliferation of printed publications, it did so in the context of a lapse in censorship control engendered by the

[15] George Puttenham, *The Arte of English Poesie* (1589), ed. G.D. Willcock and Alice Walker (Cambridge, 1936), p. 148.

absence of a clear-cut centralised authority in which the Stationers' Company could anchor its regulatory powers. For many, the pamphlet war became the anarchic enactment of civil disintegration. But it also provoked an awareness of the insecurity of the printed medium as a channel of communication, even for the author of a text like *Areopagtica*, which was arguing for – albeit limited – press freedom. The promiscuous behaviour of texts in the marketplace threatened to undermine faith in the idea of 'text' as concurrant with divine order. Textuality itself appeared unstable.

Looking back on the 1640s, Thomas Hobbes's *Leviathan* (1651) makes censorship central to its vision of the Commonwealth. Without censorship, dispute and faction in public discourse would threaten to weaken the state. Without censorship, competing interpretations of Holy Writ would fragment the unity of its significance and lead on to civil strife: it is the sovereign, and not the individual (as Milton implicitly claims in the divorce tracts), who has 'the authority of interpreting Scripture'. Ultimately, it is censorship that underpins language itself. Where words are conventional counters and bear no natural relation to the world, the linguistic system must be controlled politically at the centre – otherwise men might use words to mean whatever they want them to mean, leading to conflict and collapse. 'A sovereign is needed,' in Sharon Achinstein's words, 'to police linguistic as well as political practice' ('The Politics of Babel', p. 33). The stability of language depends, therefore, on censoring competing definitions or linguistic practices. If the absence of effective censorship appeared to destabilise textuality in the pamphlet wars of the 1640s, its presence, for Hobbes, saves the linguistic system from similar instability.

Censorship in the Manuscript Transmission
of Restoration Poetry

PAUL HAMMOND

I

Tory. But ha'ye no *Manuscripts?*
Whig. Yes I have Three cases there beyond the Chimny, that I wou'd not change for *Bodlies Library* three times over.
To. What do they treat of?
Wh. Two of 'em are altogether upon the *Art of Government,* and the *Third* is Cramm'd with *Lampoon* and *Satyr.* You sha'not name me any one Copy that has scap'd me; nor any Exigent of State; but I'le furnish ye out of these Papers with an Expedient for't.

(*The Observator* no. 110; 11 March 1682)

IN THIS EPISODE from Sir Roger L'Estrange's propaganda sheet, 'Whig' is showing 'Tory' around his library. The very existence of Whig's cache of manuscripts testifies to his seditious purposes: two whole bookcases are full of papers which allow Whig to campaign against the principles of government expounded in the officially licensed tracts, while the collection of satires preserves the work of the dissident literary imagination. L'Estrange is clearly suspicious of such a private, unofficial archive, a repository which both preserves and enables dissident thought.[1]

---

[1] For L'Estrange see George Kitchin, *Sir Roger L'Estrange: A Contribution to the History of the Press in the Seventeenth Century* (London, 1913). For the circumstances in which political poetry circulated in the Restoration see *Poems on Affairs of State,* edited by George deF. Lord et al., 7 vols. (New Haven, 1963–75), I. xxv–lvi (this collection is cited hereafter as *POAS*); Harold Love, 'Scribal Publication in Seventeenth-Century England', *Transactions of the Cambridge Bibliographical Society,* 9 (1987), pp. 130–154; Brice Harris, 'Captain Robert Julian, Secretary to the Muses', *ELH,* 10 (1943), pp. 294–309; Timothy Crist, 'Government Control of the Press after the Expiration of the Printing Act in 1679', *Publishing History,* 5 (1979), pp. 49–77; Paul Hammond, 'The Circulation of Dryden's Poetry', forthcoming in *Papers of the Bibliographical Society of America.* Unless otherwise stated, the follow-

As Surveyor of the Press, L'Estrange had devoted much of the previous twenty years to an onslaught on oppositional[2] publishing, searching the premises of writers, printers and booksellers, using spies and informers, and instigating prosecutions. The licensing of books before publication may have ensured that some dissident material never reached print, though printers and booksellers were probably more deterred by the laws of sedition and libel. Attempts to police the world of printing were never wholly successful, and after the lapsing of the Printing Act in 1679 at the height of the Popish Plot scare, there was a deluge of pamphlets opposing the policies of Charles II and his ministers. Nevertheless, the obvious dangers of printing oppositional material did promote a flourishing manuscript culture, in which scribes produced copies of the latest political and erotic poems which no printer would risk handling, but which readers who wanted to be *au courant* with public affairs were happy to lock away in their desks or transcribe into their own commonplace books.

Various literary and linguistic strategies were evolved in this world of manuscript circulation. Names of authors disappear.[3] Titles vary from copy to copy. Official tropes, the images of royal power, are parodically appropriated to oppositional causes.[4] A non-literary language of slang, jargon and obscenity is deployed, along with a repertoire of names, initials and pseudonyms to designate public figures, a vocabulary which it is easy for scribes to alter at will. Obscurity and allegory proliferate, inviting readers to bring their own interpretations to bear upon elusive texts. Many poems highlight the

ing discussion of political poetry draws upon the texts and collations printed in *POAS* vols. I–II.

[2] The terms 'oppositional' and 'dissident' are necessarily vague, since opposition to Charles and his policies came from several quarters. Ministers moved between government and 'opposition' both from principle and opportunism, and *ad hoc* alliances dominated politics until the coalescing of 'Whig' and 'Tory' groupings during the Exclusion Crisis. Most of the oppositional poems printed in *POAS* criticise Charles for tending towards Catholicism and absolutism, and for debasing the monarchy through his sexual promiscuity. In the poems of the 1660s and early 1670s there is often a vigorous republicanism which is alien to (or tactically absent from) most Whig poems of the Exclusion Crisis.

[3] See Paul Hammond, 'Anonymity in Restoration Poetry', forthcoming in *The Seventeenth Century*, 8 (1993).

[4] See Paul Hammond, 'The King's Two Bodies: Representations of Charles II' in *Culture, Politics and Society in Britain, 1660–1800*, edited by Jeremy Black and Jeremy Gregory (Manchester, 1991), pp. 13–48.

acts of speaking and writing, giving themselves a licence to criticise: authoritative names such as 'Britannia' are given to the speakers of the poems; dialogues, debates and prophetic voices are common; inscriptions of a riddling or satirical kind replace the formal inscriptions of royal power. That writers are not to be silenced becomes a major part of their subject matter. A strongly intertextual awareness was built up among readers, who became alert to the charged usage of political vocabulary (like the Whigs' claims to stand for 'liberty' and 'property') and the reusing of literary forms such as the 'Advice to a Painter' mode or 'News from Hell'. Poets like Marvell and Rochester return as ghosts to comment on the new times. In this network of poems which pass from hand to hand in the coffee houses, there is a loss of authorially-sanctioned meaning, which is replaced by a network of meanings generated by readers and scribes: hence multiple political significations become possible, and yet every interpretation is elusive, deniable.

It was into this counter-realm of oppositional writing that Dryden's *Absalom and Achitophel* intruded. Appearing anonymously, as if it needed to hide from royal displeasure, it boldly appropriated the tropes of oppositional speech through its deployment of a biblical allegory whose application is left to the reader. As Whig writers quoted and parodied the Augustan images of royal power, so Dryden now quotes and parodies the Whig rhetoric of liberty, individual judgment, common security, and the protestant heritage. In the Whig rhetorical strategies, meaning is generated liberally and communally rather than authorially and authoritatively; by quoting and parodying this poetics, *Absalom and Achitophel* is insisting upon the opposite of oppositional hermeneutics: the reader of Dryden's poem is not located by the text in the kind of position which the reader of Whig poetry would be given, with some degree of licence not only to apply the poem but even to rewrite it as he copied it out. Dryden, on the contrary, asserts that the interpretation of events which his poem produces is the definitive political text, and it is wholly appropriate that the poem circulated almost exclusively in print, with no need for manuscript copies. At the end of the poem, the ostensibly free play of speech (which has actually been a ventriloquism which usurped Whig identities, and was continually censored by the narratorial voice) ends with the single royal voice whose authority is placed beyond question or interpretation by being also the voice of God. The devices through which dissident voices spoke against royal power have now been reappropriated by the Poet Laureate on behalf of his King.

The model which seems appropriate for the understanding of 'censorship' in these circumstances, therefore, is not that of a central power which promotes orthodoxy and proscribes dissent (a model more appropriate to France under Louis XIV), but rather a network of power in which authors, scribes and readers have considerable freedom to write and circulate material, no matter how scandalous or offensive, and in which various parties struggle for rhetorical mastery, for control over both writing and reading. The scribal culture was in effect produced by the government's attempts to control printing, and it may seem to be an arena of freedom, a site of unfettered production and exchange. Yet within this system of manuscript circulation, forms of control still operated. Both readers who were making copies for their own use, and professional copyists who were transcribing to commission, exercised their own taste and judgment, producing some striking textual alterations. Readings are conflated from different texts; lines and whole passages are inserted or omitted; marginal glosses to explain the identities of the poems' targets are added or changed; attributions are attached with varying degrees of plausibility. The scribes are thus not only transmitting texts but creating new texts, and new frameworks for their interpretation. In such conditions one should think of the copyist as being also an editor, or even in some cases a second author, of the poems which he was transcribing. To these roles we can add that of censor. At this distance we cannot know who was responsible for these textual variants, and to attribute them to 'copyists' is a shorthand which probably conflates several distinct interventions which are now beyond recall. While it is unlikely that professional copyists actually composed variant passages, they certainly had considerable discretion in clarifying obscurities in their copytexts. As for censorship on moral and political grounds, it is clear that words, passages and whole poems which were acceptable to some compilers (or their employers) proved unacceptable to others; conversely, poems could also become more explicit as they were transcribed and 'improved'.

But, more broadly, 'censorship' in these circumstances is the ignoring of any claims to autonomy and authority which might be made for the original text and its author. Original intentions and meanings are overwritten by scribes who produce texts to serve the reader's purposes, whether these purposes might be political opposition or erotic stimulation. The texts, which are generally anonymous or have acquired speculative or mischievous attributions, have their marks of origin removed, and are prepared for their place not in the author's *Works* but in the reader's archive.

It is the aim of this essay to explore the kinds of censorship which operated within this manuscript circulation, first in the case of political poetry, and then in the erotic and satirical work of Rochester.

II

Some of the most damaging oppositional poetry did find its way into print: several of the *Advice to a Painter* poems which satirised the conduct of the naval war against the Dutch in 1667 circulated in printed form, partly because the profits for booksellers were high and the risks low. Even the King's bookseller, Richard Royston, had these poems on his shelves.[5] The more openly republican and more sexually explicit oppositional poems of the 1670s circulated only in manuscript, though it is noticeable that during the years 1679 to 1681 Whig printers and booksellers became much bolder in what they were prepared to publish: this may be due partly to the demise of the Printing Act, but more to the intense commitment of writers who thought the nation to be in danger from popery and arbitrary government. Whig poems which appeared in print at this period included attacks on Lord Chief Justice Scroggs (for which Jane Curtis was prosecuted), and the notorious denunciation of the King and his policies called *A Raree Show*, which included a woodcut depicting Charles as a travelling showman carrying Parliament around in a box. For this Stephen College was executed.

Some poetry critical of Charles appeared more safely in print because its target was disguised. *A Poem to the Charming Fair One* from c.1675 (Wing P2708; not in *POAS*) is an attack on the King's sexual enslavement to his French mistress the Duchess of Portsmouth, which is seen as a political enslavement to France. Her charms have defeated the English King, and so avenged England's military conquest of France. But the language of the poem is ostensibly that of a simple sexual lyric, and it has a style and rhythm which are remarkably close to Rochester's idiom:

> Yet in her pomp this wretched Fair
> Is despicably vain;
> A shrine so bright without, did ne're
> Inclose a soul so mean. (p. 1)

5 Kitchin, pp. 167–168.

Her lover exhausts Nature's store to adorn her:

> Thus Natures Treasuries unlock,
>   This Idoll to adorn:
> And from the glittering Diamond-Rock,
>   The crusted Jems are torn . . .
>
> Be frankly kinde, and pay Loves Debt!
>   Think thou'hast a King insnared:
> The Glory of a prize so great,
>   Does bring its own Reward.   (p. 2)

The trope of love as a kingdom, and lovers as royalty, is so common in Restoration erotic poetry that these verses could easily pass without a reader noticing their political charge; yet read in the light of contemporary anxiety and resentment about the Duchess's conspicuous consumption of taxes and her political influence over the King, the ostensibly innocuous verses have a disturbing force, mobilising for political purposes the rhetorical resources of the period's frightened fascination with sexually powerful women. In this case censorship has curtailed explicit speech, but promoted more complex modes of writing and interpretation.

Censorship in a different form affected some of the most outspoken manuscript poems which attack Charles directly, for several compilers evidently demurred about the terms in which the King was represented. Towards the end of the 'Fourth Advice to a Painter' (1667) there is a passage on Charles whose tone is more sarcastic and sexually explicit than the rest of the poem:

> As Nero once, with harp in hand, survey'd
> His flaming Rome and, as that burn'd, he play'd,
> So our great Prince, when the Dutch fleet arriv'd,
> Saw his ships burn'd and, as they burn'd, he swiv'd.
> So kind he was in our extremest need,
> He would those flames extinguish with his seed.
> But against Fate all human aid is vain:
> His pr-- then prov'd as useless as his chain.
>   (ll. 129–36; POAS I. 146)

This is the text as printed in the modern edition of *Poems on Affairs of State* from Bodleian MS Eng. Poet.e.4, but other early witnesses tell a different story. The complete passage is omitted from three manuscripts, while the last four lines, the most sexually explicit ones, are omitted from the contemporary printed text, *Directions to a Painter*

(1667). Other manuscripts illustrate the freedom with which sexual vocabulary was altered, as they replace 'prick' with 'swiving' or 'fucking'. Similarly, a manuscript of 'A Ballad called the Haymarket Hectors' cuts out a reference to Charles 'consulting his cazzo', and substitutes a comment on his liking 'for sweet variety' (POAS I. 169–171).

Notable amongst the variations for reasons of sexual decorum is a tendency to eliminate references to sodomy (whether homosexual or heterosexual). 'Further Advice to a Painter' (POAS I. 164–167) begins with a comparison of Charles II and the Roman emperor Commodus, which says that at night they repair 'One to his pathic, the other to his play'r' (l. 10). One manuscript changes 'pathic' to 'punk', even though the reference here is to Commodus, not to Charles. A line in 'Nostradamus' Prophecy' (POAS I. 186–189) claiming that 'sodomy is the Prime Minister's sport' (l. 17; referring to the Duke of Buckingham) is changed from 'sodomy' to 'so doing', a variant which can be explained both as a misreading of the handwriting in the copy which the scribe was working from, and as a rewriting on grounds of taste. And in 'Last Instructions to a Painter' (POAS I. 99–139) the line 'Bugger'd in incest with the mongrel beast' (l. 146) was too strong for the copyist who changed 'bugger'd' to 'proceeds'. (Incest and bestiality apparently caused him no problem.)

Blasphemy was another reason for scribes censoring the poems that they copied. 'The Downfall of the Chancellor' has a couplet which one manuscript omits, probably because of its invocation of God:

> God is reveng'd too for the stones he took
> From aged Paul's to make a nest for th' rook.
> (ll. 11–12; POAS I. 158)

In 'Britannia and Raleigh' the line attacking the Duke of York's adherence to Roman Catholicism:

> Mac James the Irish pagod does adore:
> (l. 125; POAS I. 233)

appears in many texts with 'pagod' changed to 'bigots': this is plausible palaeographically, but it also removes the suggestion that the Catholics' God is a pagan idol. 'The Royal Buss' comments that as in ancient times there was a struggle between the gods and the giants, so now there is a struggle between Parliament and the Court:

> But, bless'd be Jove, the gods of ours
> Are greater in their guilt than pow'rs.
> Though then the heathens were such fools,
> Yet they made gods of better tools.
>
> (ll. 5–8; POAS I. 263)

One manuscript omits the last two lines, perhaps from a sensitivity about the idea of making gods. Though one can never confidently assign motives for such misreading (or creative rereading), it does seem as if sexual and religious sensibilities prompted the production of textual variants which were in effect small acts of censorship within this arena which was specifically devoted to 'free' speech.

Of all the political poems from the reign of Charles II, one of the most notorious (and one of the most unstable textually) was the Earl of Rochester's lampoon on Charles II.[6] This was subjected to considerable alteration in transmission, with the order of the lines being changed, some of the more explicit sexual details omitted, and some passages being rewritten: indeed, so radical are the differences between the extant manuscripts that it is impossible to reconstruct the original text with any confidence. This makes comment on the direction of scribal revision hazardous, but some revealing features of the transmission can nevertheless be illustrated. Several variants suggest a nervousness about the poem. The title is sometimes given as 'On the King', sometimes simply as 'A Satyr'; other titles take an anecdotal form – 'On K: C: IId by the E of Roch___r; For which he was banish'd the Court, and turn'd Mountebank' – or they pass a judgment: 'A base Copy'. In the text which David M. Vieth prints (Bodleian MS Rawl. D. 924) the poem is clearly set in the present:

> Their Reigns (& oh Long May hee Reigne . . .

But other texts awkwardly try to disguise the contemporaneity:

---

6 For a text see *The Complete Poems of John Wilmot, Earl of Rochester*, edited by David M. Vieth (New Haven, 1968), pp. 60–61. The manuscripts of this poem are listed in *The Poems of John Wilmot, Earl of Rochester*, edited by Keith Walker (Oxford, 1984), p. 185. Neither Vieth nor Walker provides a collation for this poem, and the collation in POAS I. 479–480 is inadequate, though it does give a sense of the problem. Vieth discusses the poem in 'Rochester's "Scepter" Lampoon on Charles II', PQ, 37 (1958), pp. 424–432. The Yale MS is quoted here from Vieth's article, the others from my own transcriptions; the variant titles are quoted from Walker's textual notes.

Not long since reign'd oh may he long survive.
(BL MS Harley 7317)

Some versions report the King's lament to his mistress:

> To Carwell y^e. Most Deare of all his Deares
> The Best Releiffe of his Declining yeares
> Offt he Bewayles his fortune & her fate
> (Bodleian MS Rawl. D. 924)

whereas others more boldly cast this into direct speech, showing no qualms about usurping the King's voice:

> Ah my deare Carwell, dearest of my Deares,!
> Thou best Releife of my declineing yeares!
> O How I mourne thy Fortune & My Fate.
> (BL MS Harley 7315)

Rochester's account of the King's liking for ease above all (and one kind of ease in particular) has a sharp epigrammatic force in some texts:

> Peace was his Aime, his gentleness was such
> And love, he lov'd, for he lou'd fucking much.
> (Leeds University Library Brotherton Collection MS Lt 54)

But other texts (through anxiety, perhaps, about what they are saying) scramble the second line in various ways:

> That as his Loue is Great, he swiues as much
> (Bodleian MS Rawl. D. 924)

> And's Loue, for he lou'd fucking much.
> (Bodleian MS Don. b. 8)

> Oh how he lov'd, Oh he lov'd fucking much
> (BL MS Harley 7317)

> And those he Loves, he loves for f____ much
> (Yale MS Osborn Chest II, Number 1)

The couplet which so vividly encapsulates the King's degeneracy:

> Who restless rowles ab^t. from whore to whore,
> Grown impotent & scandalously poor.
>
> (BL MS Add 23722)

is also found as a triplet:

> Restlesse he Rowles about from Whore to Whore
> With Dogg & Bastard, alwayes going before,
> A merry Monarch, scandalous & poore
>
> (BL MS Harley 7315)

(where the tone is attractively complex in that third line); and in yet another version as four lines:

> Restlesse he roues from whore to whore,
> An easy Monarch, scandalous, & poore.
> With a damn'd crue to whores he joggs
> Of Bastards, Pimps, Buffoones, & Dogs.
>
> (Bodleian MS Don. b. 8)

Here the phrasing is cruder, the tone more cruel. This version is a more outspoken piece of political opposition. The political character of the poem is also shifted by the different positions assigned to this explicitly republican couplet:

> I hate all Monarchs & the Thrones they sitt on,
> From ye Hector of France to ye Cully of Brittain
>
> (BL MS Add 23722)

which is sometimes placed in the middle of the poem, sometimes more emphatically at the end.

Without being able to reconstruct Rochester's original text we cannot give a precise account of the way in which the poem was rewritten in transmission; but it is clear that many scribes, readers and would-be satirists tried their hands at improving the piece as it was passed around, changing its tone, its sexual explicitness and its political charge. The very fact that the original text is lost and replaced by a bewildering array of versions, is a striking example of scribal censorship: 'censorship' here is not simply the removing or rephrasing of offensive material (though that is clearly happening) but the recasting of the poem, its appropriation to a variety of new emphases. It is significant that the most outrageous satire on Charles II should be a *locus* of special textual difficulty, for this extraordinarily transgressive writing seems to have inhibited some of the copyists, while for others it liberated their own imaginations to extend and rework what they had set out simply to transcribe. Indeed, so radical are the changes which were made to this poem that in some cases the text is likely to have been produced not by transcription from a written copy, but by memorial reconstruction. The memory easily retains couplets, but not always in their original order – particularly when a poem's structure is so slight – and couplets may be changed to triplets, or *vice versa*, in the act of writing down what is half-remembered. Typical of memorial reconstruction too is the ability to recall the main point of a line, but not its precise phrasing. This poem was probably too transgressive for some people to be comfortable about handling written copies, and so it was committed to memory and only later confided to paper in moments of privacy. Thus the fear of authority drove readers to guard this poem in that most secret of archives, their memories, where it was metamorphosed into that form which most suited the readers by whom it was half-recalled, half-created.

III

After the revolution of 1688 many of the political poems which had circulated only in manuscript during the reigns of Charles II and James II appeared in printed collections of poems on affairs of state, several of which advertised on their title pages that they contained poems 'against popery and tyranny'. Ostensibly the tyranny of official censorship which had kept such pieces from being printed and published freely had now been broken. But an examination of the variants between the texts as printed in these anthologies and those from the original manuscript circulation shows that many of these poems were censored to remove sensitive material, presumably by compilers responding to the criteria of political correctness under the new regime. This amounts to a rewriting of the oppositional poetry from the time of Charles II in the light of what the Whig cause had subsequently become. Though the parliamentary Whig opposition to Charles' government had sought only to modify the constitutional arrangement for the succession so as to preserve protestant liberties, there had been a strong republican element in the Whig coalition which made its voice heard with particular force in manuscript poetry. It is striking that this radical component of early Whiggism is removed from the poems which are collected to create a Whig canon after 1688.

'The History of Insipids', from 1674, is a catalogue of the King's mismanagement which makes Charles personally responsible for the errors and disasters of his reign, and yet the printed texts of 1689 and 1697 tone down the poem in an effort to spare Charles (and by extension other English kings) some of the more damaging charges. One stanza, which in early sources appears as:

> The wolf of France and British goat,
>   One Europe's scorn, t'other her curse
> (This fool, that knave, by public vote,
>   Yet hard to say which is the worse),
> To think such kings, Lord, reign by thee
> Were most prodigious blasphemy. (ll. 145–50; POAS I. 250)

is rewritten to exclude Charles and make Louis XIV the sole example of bad kingship; in the printed texts the first four lines become:

> That false, rapacious wolf of France,
>   The scourge of Europe and its curse,
> Who at his subjects' cry does dance,
>   And study how to make them worse.   (POAS I. 466)

The same texts change 'Charles' to 'James' (1. 34), 'Charles and Louis' to 'treacherous Louis' (1. 141), and remove the republican threat in 'Turn'd commonwealth, we will abhor you' (1. 138) by changing it to the innocuous 'Grown wise by wrongs we shall abhor you'. Some of the more explicit lines on the King's sexual behaviour in 'Colin', 'The King's Answer' and 'Hodge' were also removed when the poems were printed in 1689, though present in the previous manuscripts.

'A Dialogue between the Two Horses' (the horses from the equestrian statues of Charles I and Charles II) comes to a climax in these lines:

> Then England rejoice, thy redemption draws nigh:
> Thy oppression together with kingship shall die!
> A commonwealth! a commonwealth! we proclaim to the nation,
> For the gods have repented the King's Restoration.
>   (ll. 159–62; POAS I. 282)

Though present in the manuscripts which preserve the poem as it first circulated in 1676, these lines are omitted by the printed texts from the reign of William III. Other alterations similarly remove republican

sentiment: the prospect of 'monarchy's downfall' (l. 169) is changed
to 'tyranny's downfall', while a reference to the 'crimes' of tyrants is
softened into 'faults' (l. 176). Also omitted is the couplet which
concludes the discussion in which monarchs are characterised as
either cruel like Nero or lecherous and lazy like Sardanapalus:

> One of the two tyrants must still be our case
> Under all that shall reign of the false Scottish race.
> (ll. 135–6)

Since one member of that false Scottish race of Stuarts was currently
on the throne as Mary II, these lines were cut from the printed edition
of 1689 (but not, curiously, from that of 1697, after her death).
Similar censorship cut out the discussion of the Stuarts in 'Britannia
and Raleigh'. Britannia makes a powerful denunciation of Stuart
tyranny:

> Raleigh, no more; too long in vain I've tried
> The Stuart from the tyrant to divide . . .
> And shall this stinking Scottish brood evade
> Eternal laws, by God for mankind made?
> (ll. 141–2; 153–4; POAS I. 234)

These lines are cut out in the 1689 edition, and the last two lines are
also omitted in the 1697 text.

A bizarre allegation in 'Hodge' (1679) that Mary was married to
William of Orange in order to introduce popery to the Netherlands,
was removed from the poem as printed in 1689, depriving readers of
these lines:

> His pocky brat, got on adult'rous Nan,
> With Orange join'd the Belgians to trepan,
> Goes to The Hague for the same holy end
> As Rome to us does spurious Este send.
> (ll. 68–71; POAS II. 148)

It is understandable that a publisher in 1689 might think it unwise to
describe Queen Mary in print as a 'pocky brat' and her mother as an
adultress. Similar sensitivities caused alterations in the text of 'An
Historical Poem' from 1680. An uncomplimentary reference to Mary,
Princess of Orange (mother of William III) is removed from the 1689
text:

> And his Dutch sister quickly after di'd,
> Soft in her nature and of wanton pride.
>
> (ll. 19–20; *POAS* II. 155–6)

These lines are followed by the allegation that Anne Hyde (mother of Mary II) was pregnant by the Earl of Falmouth when she married James Duke of York:

> Bold James survives, no dangers make him flinch,
> He marri'd Mynheer Falmouth's pregnant wench.
>
> (ll. 21–22)

In the 1689 text these lines are replaced by the politically safer reflection on James' political role:

> Bold Y__k survives to be the nation's curse
> Resolv'd to ruin it by deceit or force.

The same text then omits the following passage on Queen Henrietta Maria, who as grandmother of Mary II was evidently also an unsuitable target for abuse in the new reign. A later reference to 'the ill-got race of Stuarts' (l. 57) is altered to omit 'ill-got', while the 1697 edition prudently changes 'ill-got' to 'royal'.

The rewriting of Whiggism which these texts offer is also seen in their treatment of the first generation of Whig heroes. 'A Charge to the Grand Inquest of England, 1674' is a piece of pro-government satire which blames the parliamentary opposition for encroaching on the royal prerogative. Many members of the opposition are named, but in the 1697 edition two names are changed: in the line

> Temple and Marvell, who yet wears his ears
>
> (l. 10; *POAS* I. 222)

the name 'Marvell' is changed to 'S_____', while in the line

> Ransack your writers, Milton, Needham, Prynne;   (l. 42)

'Milton' is replaced by 'Selden'. It looks as if the reputations of these two major champions of the Whig cause are being protected by careful censorship.

IV

Censorship of the erotic and sexually explicit poems of the Earl of Rochester began in his lifetime and lasted into the 1960s.[7] Two poems ('The Imperfect Enjoyment' and 'A Ramble in St James' Park') were omitted from Vivian de Sola Pinto's edition of Rochester (first published in 1953 with a second edition in 1964) at the publisher's request, for fear of prosecution. Some of the texts which Pinto does print are affected by a much earlier form of censorship, since for several poems he uses the edition published by Jacob Tonson in 1691, in which many poems were bowdlerised by the alteration of the vocabulary, and the omission of whole lines and stanzas. One might expect Tonson, who was the leading literary publisher of his age, to issue a text which had been made verbally decent and visually sober, and was clearly distanced from both the scruffy 'Antwerp' editions of Rochester and the connoisseurs' luxury manuscripts. But the scribes who produced those manuscripts had their own moral and aesthetic criteria which often affected the process of transcription.

The selection of material for inclusion in manuscript miscellanies might not seem to merit the description of 'censorship', but the process of assembly determined which poems were read together as a group, and therefore suggested a framework of interpretation for individual poems, as well as fashioning a canon, and therefore an image, for Rochester. A substantial group of his erotic poems is found together in the Gyldenstolpe manuscript (a richly bound collection written by a professional scribe for a wealthy reader around 1680),[8] and in virtually the same order in other similar manuscripts from the same date. The inclusion of Rochester's translation fron Seneca's *Troades* ('After death nothing is, and nothing, death . . .') between 'The Disabled Debauchee' and 'The Imperfect Enjoyment' implies that this should be read as a libertine poem, thus reducing its

---

[7] Rochester is quoted from Vieth's edition, but the variant readings are taken from Walker's collations. Badminton MS FmE 3/12, not known to Vieth or Walker, is quoted by kind permission of the Duke of Somerset; a calendar and discussion of this manuscript by Michael Brennan and Paul Hammond is forthcoming in *English Manuscript Studies*.

[8] This has been published in facsimile: *The Gyldenstolpe Manuscript Miscellany of Poems by John Wilmot, Earl of Rochester, and other Restoration Authors*, edited by Bror Danielsson and David M. Vieth, Stockholm Studies in English, 17 (Stockholm, 1967).

philosophical seriousness and turning it into a piece of fashionable
sceptical posturing. Conversely, the quotations from Rochester in the
writings of Charles Blount give the poetry a more serious philosophical status.[9] Because poems by (or associated with) Rochester often
circulated in small groups,[10] variations in the composition of the
groups clearly reveal editorial intervention: a case in point is the
unpleasant and crudely explicit poem 'Advice to a Cunt Monger'
which appears in Badminton MS FmE 3/12 as part of a sequence of
poems which is replicated exactly in the Gyldenstolpe MS except for
the omission of this piece.

The structural alteration of these small canons of erotic poetry is
one instance of the taste and sensibilities of the copyists, but the
structure of individual poems is also manipulated. The song 'Fair
Chloris in a pigsty lay' evidently disturbed some copyists. Chloris
dreams first that one of her pigs is stuck in the entrance to a cave, and
then that she is being penetrated by a local swain:

> Now pierced is her virgin zone;
>   She feels the foe within it.
> She hears a broken amorous groan,
> The panting lover's fainting moan,
>   Just in the happy minute.
>
> Frighted she wakes, and waking frigs.
>   Nature thus kindly eased
> In dreams raised by her murmuring pigs
> And her own thumb between her legs,
>   She's innocent and pleased.   (ll. 31–40)

Tonson's edition of 1691 omits the last stanza, but prints the previous
one; Yale MS Osborn PB. VI/88 omits both, along with the preceding
stanza. In the case of 'To a Lady, in a Letter' Tonson's edition orig-
inally printed a full text of the poem, but this was subsequently
cancelled and replaced by a shorter text.[11] Other poems are contained
and made respectable not by excision but by addition: the yielding of
Chloris to the shepherd in the song 'As Chloris full of harmless

---

9 See Gillian Manning, 'Some Quotations from Rochester in Charles
Blount's *Philostratus*', *Notes and Queries*, 231 (1986), 38–40.
10 See David M. Vieth, *Attribution in Restoration Poetry* (New Haven, 1963).
11 See David M. Vieth, 'A Textual Paradox: Rochester's "To a Lady in a
Letter" ', *Papers of the Bibliographical Society of America*, 54, (1960), pp.
147–162, and 'An Unsuspected Cancel in Tonson's 1691 "Rochester" ',
Papers of the Bibliographical Society of America, 55 (1961), pp. 130–133.

thought' is enclosed within a new narrative framework when the poem is printed in the broadside *Corydon and Cloris* [1676]. But structural alteration is not always carried out in the interests of decorum: indeed, the use of stanzas or couplets in most Restoration poems, together with their often casual design, seem to have encouraged other writers to add material of their own which extends rather than constrains the original. The verses on 'Signior Dildo', which describe the reactions of various court ladies to the arrival of this useful implement, appear in a different order in different manuscripts, and acquire additional stanzas in Bodleian MS Don.b.8 which introduce further characters into the satire. In BL MS Harley 7312 Rochester's self-dramatising poem 'To the Postboy' is joined to the poem usually called 'One writing against his prick' to produce not only a new version of Rochester's poem but a new version of his persona.[12] And in Leeds Brotherton Collection MS Lt q 52 'Upon Nothing' is made into a dialogue between Rochester, Buckingham and Fleetwood Shepherd.[13]

It is again at the level of verbal variants that one can see the operation of the scribe as censor, for those who copied out Rochester's most explicit poems would at some points decide to intervene and tone down the text. In the case of 'The Disabled Debauchee' four manuscripts omit four stanzas, and two omit three stanzas (though not exactly the same ones). The stanza which caused most concern was the following, where the male speaker recalls his contest with Cloris over which of them would bed the servant boy:

> Nor shall our love-fits, Cloris, be forgot,
> When each the well-looked linkboy strove t'enjoy,
> And the best kiss was the deciding lot
> Whether the boy fucked you, or I the boy.   (ll. 37–40)

This is the text which appears in Vieth's edition, based on Yale MS Osborn b. 105. Tonson's edition omits this stanza, as do seven of the fourteen manuscripts recorded in Keith Walker's edition (one actually has the stanza number followed by a gap). Moreover, several of those manuscripts which do include the stanza alter the wording: two manuscripts change 'well-looked' to 'best loved'; the same two witnesses plus a third omit 'boy' altogether; two others tone down the sexual contest by changing 'strove' to 'sought'. In the last line the Yale

---

[12] See John D. Patterson, 'Another Text of Rochester's "To the Post Boy" ', *Restoration*, 4 (1980) pp. 14–16.
[13] Illustrated as plates 6 and 7 in *The Seventeenth Century*, 8 (1993).

MS and the printed collection called *Poems on Several Occasions By
the Right Honourable, the E. of R___* (ostensibly published in Antwerp
in 1680) read 'us'd' for 'fucked', while Bodleian MS Don.b.8 makes a
muddled attempt to remove the homosexual element by replacing 'I'
with 'you' in the last line.

   This reticence about homosexual intercourse is found elsewhere in
the textual transmission of Rochester's poems. The song which begins
'Love a woman? you're an ass!' ends with the lines:

> . . . if busy love entrenches,
> There's a sweet, soft page of mine
> Does the trick worth forty wenches.

This stanza was omitted in the 1691 edition, but only after the page
on which the full text had been printed was cancelled, and a replacement
leaf substituted which removed the offending lines.[14] 'The Imperfect
Enjoyment' is an explicit poem which generally suffers little interference
from scribal censorship, and yet a couple of lines from Rochester's
denunciation of his wayward penis did prompt some alteration:

> Stiffly resolved, 'twould carelessly invade
> Woman or man, nor ought its fury stayed:
> Where'er it pierced, a cunt it found or made –   (ll. 41–3)

The copyist of Badminton MS FmE 3/12 seems to have found
'pierced' too explicit, and changed it to 'pressed'. The 1680 edition
changes 'man' to 'boy', altering the homosexual encounter from that
of two adults to that of adult and boy, apparently a more acceptable
(because more classical?) form of homosexual relationship.

   In 'An Allusion to Horace' some copyists were offended by Rochester's obscene remarks on Dryden. This is how the lines appear in
Vieth's edition:

> Dryden in vain tried this nice way of wit,
> For he to be a tearing blade thought fit.
> But when he would be sharp, he still was blunt:
> To frisk his frolic fancy, he'd cry "Cunt!"
> Would give the ladies a dry bawdy bob,
> And thus he got the name of Poet Squab.   (ll. 71–6)

---

14 See Vieth, 'An Unsuspected Cancel', p. 131 n. 2.

Several scribes recoil from this denigration of Dryden: Bodleian MS Rawl. Poet. 19 omits lines 73–4, while Cambridge University Library MS Add. 42 omits lines 73–6; several manuscripts replace 'Cunt' with a dash; and Bodleian MS Add. B 106 substitutes 'coy modest' for 'dry bawdy'. However, copyists are still capable of adding their own crudity to Rochester's: BL MS Sloane 1504 reads 'frig' for 'frisk'.

The fear of blasphemy also prompted some acts of censorship. Scribes who happily copied out the explicit sexual details of 'A Ramble in St James' Park' balked at lines which used religious language in an irreverent context:

> But though St. James has th' honor on 't,
> 'Tis consecrate to prick and cunt.   (ll. 9–10)

These lines are omitted from BL MS Harley 6057, while Edinburgh University Library MS DC.1.3 omits the later lines which describe the impossible things which will come to pass before the poet ceases to seek revenge on his unfaithful mistress:

> Crab-louse, inspired with grace divine,
> From earthly cod to heaven shall climb;
> Physicians shall believe in Jesus,
> And disobedience cease to please us.   (ll. 147–50)

Curiously, this scribe had no qualms about including the *adynaton* which immediately precedes line 147:

> The Jesuits' fraternity
> Shall leave the use of buggery;   (ll. 145–6)

Was this because the allegation belonged to the repertoire of contemporary political jibes rather than to a primarily religious discourse?

V

If political and erotic poetry prompted most of the scribes' anxious rewritings, there were nevertheless other poems by Rochester which attracted intervention. *Tunbridge Wells*, with its loose structure and unfocussed satire, is one of the most chaotic of Rochester's poems textually, and seems to have lent itself to the addition and rearrangement of material *ad libitum*.[15] Several passages appear to have been added to the original poem, probably in several different stages of revision. Disentangling these now seems a forlorn task, so one example must serve to illustrate the state of the text. The description of the foolish visitor to the spa is printed by Vieth as follows:

> From coach and six a thing unwieldy rolled,
> Whose lumber, cart more decently would hold.
> As wise as calf it looked, as big as bully,
> But handled, proves a mere Sir Nicholas Cully;
> A bawling fop, a natural Nokes, and yet
> He dares to censure as if he had wit.
> To make him more ridiculous, in spite
> Nature contrived the fool should be a knight.   [18]
> Though he alone were dismal sight enough,
> His train contributed to set him off,
> All of his shape, all of the selfsame stuff.
> No spleen or malice need on them be thrown:
> Nature has done the business of lampoon,
> And in their look their characters has shown.   (ll. 11–24)

After line 18, Yale MS Osborn b. 105 has the following lines:

> Grant yee unlucky Starrs, this oregrowne Boy,
> To purchase some inspireing pretty Toy
> That may his want of Sense, and Witt supply,
> As Buxome Crabb-fish, does his Lechery.

Three witnesses omit this passage: have they dropped it, or have the other texts added it? After line 24, at the end of the passage quoted, the Yale MS has:

> Thrice blest be he, who Dildoe did invent!
> To ramm the Neighb'ring hole to Fundament;
> Which may be lengthen'd, thicken'd, in its measure,
> And us'd at Lech'rous ugly Trullas pleasure:
> For ne're was Bulke, or Stomach giv'n to Tarses,
> Either to fill, or smell such Foggy Arses.

This time six manuscripts omit these lines; do they represent a censored text, or do the others preserve an addition which was written in

---

[15] Vieth and Walker print substantially different texts of this poem. For a critique of Walker's decisions see my review of his edition in *RES*, 37 (1986), pp. 263–265.

to make the poem more salacious? What is certain is that after the poem had been transcribed into Bodleian MS Don.f.29 this latter passage was scored out, probably on grounds not of textual authenticity but of decency, since a later couplet on the sexual potency of Cuff and Kick, and a passage attacking the clergy, are also scored through.

Philosophical argument caused problems for copyists of Rochester's 'Satire against Reason and Mankind'. Some manuscripts predictably omit lines which satirise the clergy, for example:

> . . . that sensual tribe whose talents lie
> In avarice, pride, sloth, and gluttony;
> Who hunt good livings but abhor good lives . . .
>
> (ll. 198–200)

But more interesting is the problem which copyists have with the paradoxes which are typical of the poem's style of argument. The difficult, compact argument in the line:

> And therefore what they fear at heart, they hate. (l. 45)

proved too difficult for the scribe of BL MS Harley 7312, who simply left it out, while relics of another struggle with the line can be seen in the variant reading 'least' for 'heart' in the 1680 editions, with the further variant 'last' for 'least' in some manuscripts. The bold paradox:

> For all men would be cowards if they durst. (l. 158)

defeated the copyist of BL MS Sloane 1458, who changed 'cowards' into 'noble'. Similarly, the line:

> Most men are cowards, all men should be knaves (l. 169)

puzzled the copyist of the Illinois MS, who left it out, and the scribe of National Library of Scotland MS 2201, who turned it back towards the familiar association of knaves and fools by changing 'cowards' to 'fools'. The philosophical vocabulary of the poem is similarly altered throughout by scribes who find Rochester's style and diction too demanding. A few examples will illustrate the point: 'instinct' becomes 'instance' (l. 10); 'doubts' becomes 'thoughts' (l. 19); 'profess' becomes 'suppose' or 'confess' or 'protest' (l. 53); 'aspiring' becomes 'inspiring' (l. 66); 'bounds' becomes 'binds' (l. 102); 'distinction' becomes 'discretion' (l. 110); 'true' becomes 'right' (l. 111); 'passion' becomes 'actions' (l. 143). And there is one small but telling case of Rochester's sceptical argument being appropriated for orthodox religion when the line 'Huddled in dirt the reasoning engine lies' (l. 29) is given a conventional biblical resonance by the alteration of 'dirt' to 'dust'.

Several passages in which the argument is particularly condensed or paradoxical are abbreviated or rewritten; one example is the comparison of man and dog:

> For all his pride and his philosophy,
> 'Tis evident beasts are, in their degree,   [115]
> As wise at least, and better far than he.
> Those creatures are the wisest who attain,
> By surest means, the ends at which they aim.
> If therefore Jowler finds and kills his hares
> Better than Meres supplies committee chairs,   [120]
> Though one's a statesman, th' other but a hound,
> Jowler, in justice, would be wiser found.
>   You see how far man's wisdom here extends;
> Look next if human nature makes amends:
> Whose principles most generous are, and just,   [125]
> And to whose morals you would sooner trust.
> Be judge yourself, I'll bring it to the test:
> Which is the basest creature, man or beast?   (ll. 114–28)

This passage caused a considerable amount of confusion. The text in National Library of Wales Ottley papers omits all but the last couplet; BL MS Sloane 1458 omits the first line and lines 119–26; Bodleian MS Add. B. 106 transposes lines 121–2; the Illinois MS omits line 126. In the last line 'basest' appears in various witnesses as 'baser', 'noblest', 'vilest', 'wisest' or 'bravest', or is omitted altogether: evidently both the logic and the tone of Rochester's argument defeated many of these early readers. Indeed, so disconcerting was Rochester's argument that eight lines which try to explain it are added after line 122 in BL MS Harley 7312:

> ffor Jowler finds, and kills; Reason's his Cause
> But Statesmen's reason's grounded upon Laws
> Which Contradict right reason in us hence
> Hee fondly makes the Senses Clash with sence
> ffor ask from whence the Lawes, do take their rise
> T'is answ'd Sence right reasons Paradice
> Jowler you see dispatch't, but you must Tarry
> Till the Greek Kalends, for the Statesman's Quarry.

What we see here is not simply perplexity in the face of a difficult and sometimes slackly-argued poem (though that is part of the problem) but an attempt to contain the poem's challenge to a complacent orthodoxy by spoiling its sharp paradoxes and uncomfortable ironies. The rebuttal of Rochester's poem was not conducted only in the formal rejoinders which were published: it began in the very transmission of the poem itself.

VI

On 8 February 1668 Samuel Pepys bought a copy of the pornographic tale *L'escholle des Filles* 'in plain binding (avoiding the buying of it better bound) because I resolve, as soon as I have read it, to burn it, that it may not stand in the list of books, nor among them, to disgrace them if it should be found.' The next day, which was a Sunday, he retired to his chamber, and read the book 'for information sake (But it did hazer my prick para stand all the while, and una vez to decharger)'. He then burnt it.[16] There is something engagingly paradoxical about Pepys as censor. He reads the book in private; makes sure that it is not found by others in his library or recorded in its catalogue; and uses a macaronic private language to conceal his orgasm. But it is all recorded in the diary, which is only a temporarily private repository: the language is easily decoded. The censor ensures that both the act and its concealment leave their traces. Later, when Pepys acquired a copy of the 1680 edition of Rochester, he added its obscenities to his library; he had it bound up with two other texts, a manuscript supplement of ten further poems by Rochester or associated with his rakish milieu, and Gilbert Burnet's *Some Passages of the Life and Death of the Right Honourable John, Earl of Rochester*. It is a nicely ambivalent gesture: the poems are preserved, but are also framed by the bishop's orthodox commentary on Rochester and his way of life.

The archives which readers built up made these manuscript poems into their own property: the Gyldenstolpe manuscript became a luxury item in the Royal Library in Stockholm; the Badminton manuscript linked the poems with other material useful in a nobleman's study – details of the royal household, constitutional notes, and legal memoranda on the New Forest. John Oldham's transcripts of

[16] *The Diary of Samuel Pepys*, edited by Robert Latham and William Matthews, 11 vols. (1970–83), IX. 57–59.

Rochester (Bodleian MS Rawl. Poet. 123) were shuffled in amongst working drafts of his own poetry, forming a physical symbol of the unresolved engagement with Rochester which characterised his work. The political circumstances which forced writers to resort to manuscript circulation enabled them to speak more forcefully than they could ever have done in print: censorship empowered writers. But the conditions of transmission also empowered readers, who selected, edited and rewrote the material which interested them: manuscript circulation unlocked the creativity of readers by removing poetry from the fixity and dignity of print, with its claims for definitive authority. Virtually none of this poetry survives in authorial autograph manuscripts: this is a world without originals but full of multiple copies, every one unique; there are no authors but many redactors; no single controlling royal power, but a multitude of fractious and irreverent citizens. The death of the author is the birth of many censors.

Faking it: Shakespeare and the 1790s

JONATHAN BATE

> 'Every thing, Sir, now-a-days has to do
> with Shakespeare: the difficulty is, to
> find out what has not to do with him.'[1]

THE WORKS OF SHAKESPEARE have had many brushes with the censor. In the playwright's own lifetime, the deposition scene was excised from printed editions of *Richard II*; in 1738 the editor and printer of *The Craftsman* were arrested for making seditious applications of a collection of passages from the history plays;[2] in the early nineteenth century Henrietta and Thomas Bowdler cleaned up the Works for family use (the problem of creating a sex-free text of *Measure for Measure* proved so intractable that they gave up and simply omitted the play from the *Family Shakespeare*). The censor is at his busiest in times of war and political unrest. Both these conditions prevailed in the 1790s, and the history of some of the time's key texts – most notably Tom Paine's *Rights of Man* – is one of continual encounters with various forms of censorship. To my knowledge, the works of Shakespeare had no such direct encounter during that decade, but in this essay I will suggest that some of the arguments about and around them amounted to censorship by other means.

In arguing this, it will become possible to dissent from a position which has been strongly articulated in two recent books. In his sprightly, contentious history of Shakespeare's cultural afterlife from the Restoration to the present, Gary Taylor proposes a link between the dramatist's canonicity and the absence of an English Revolution in the 1790s:

> Shakespeare was not deposed *because* George III was not deposed; or, George III was not deposed *because* Shakespeare was not deposed. From 1790 on, the defense of political and social privilege was justified as a defense of the culture of the English people, and

---

[1] George Hardinge, *Chalmeriana: or a Collection of Papers literary and political* (London, 1800), p. 20.

[2] See my *Shakespearean Constitutions: Politics, Theatre, Criticism 1730–1830* (Oxford, 1989), pp. 68–70.

any such defense would inevitably entail the preservation of Shakespeare, already widely regarded as England's greatest artist. Indeed, Shakespeare was certain to be further glorified by such a movement.[3]

According to this analysis, Shakespeare's principal function in English culture since the mid-eighteenth century has been to serve the Establishment by upholding traditional values and standing as the embodiment of England's greatness. Taylor follows cultural materialists like Alan Sinfield in pointing to the name of our most well-established national theatre company and saying 'there, I told you so': the *Royal* Shakespeare Company.[4]

If Taylor's argument is correct, then there was no reason to censor Shakespeare on political grounds after 1790 – all that was required was the Bowdlers' moral intervention in the name of middle-class family values. Why was 1790 a watershed? The second recent book, Margreta de Grazia's *Shakespeare Verbatim*, proposes that it was because Edmond Malone's edition, published that year, reconstructed Shakespeare in a new and highly influential way which led to a hidden political end – in essence, Malone invented what we may call bourgeois Shakespeare, and it is an English bourgeois that Shakespeare has remained for two hundred years.[5]

In 1790 an Irish-born scholar and an Irish-born statesman exchanged presentation copies of their recent works: Edmond Malone's *Plays and Poems of William Shakspeare* and Edmund Burke's *Reflections on the Revolution in France*. Six years later Burke commended Malone for his politics and his scholarship in the same breath: 'Your admiration of Shakspeare would be ill sorted indeed, if your Taste (to talk of nothing else) did not lead you to a perfect abhorrence of the French Revolution, and all its Works'.[6] Malone's edition was first of all Burkean in its treatment of Shakespeare's life: the introductory material played down the 'folk' image of Shakespeare, transmitted via oral tradition – the undisciplined youth stealing deer from Sir Thomas

---

3 Gary Taylor, *Reinventing Shakespeare: A Cultural History from the Restoration to the Present* (London, 1989), p. 149.
4 See Sinfield's contributions to *Political Shakespeare: New Essays in Cultural Materialism*, edited by him with Jonathan Dollimore (Manchester, 1986).
5 De Grazia, *Shakespeare Verbatim: The Reproduction of Authenticity and the 1790 Apparatus* (Oxford, 1991).
6 Letter to Malone, 5 April 1796, in *The Correspondence of Edmund Burke*, 10 vols. (Cambridge, 1958–78), vol. 8, ed. R. B. McDowell (1969), p. 456.

Lucy's Charlecote Park – and brought forward instead a series of documents concerning his business dealings, for instance a conveyance proving that he purchased a house in Blackfriars from one Henry Walker in 1613. The National Poet thus ceased to be a man of the people, careless of authority, and was recreated as an impeccable bourgeois gentleman, busily accumulating property and respectability in London and Stratford. With this image, Malone, like Burke, provided some much-needed comfort for the higher and middling orders of society, threatened as they were by events across the Channel. That Shakespeare was a Man of Property guaranteed the principle that private property was sacred. We need look no further than our wallets to see how influential Malone's move has been: what is it that guarantees the authenticity of the card that guarantees the authenticity of our cheques? A hologram of Shakespeare's head. The Bard smiles on the capitalist banking system.

But Malone was even more thoroughgoingly Burkean in his editorial practice: previous eighteenth-century editors, with the exception of the marginalised Capell, had concentrated on *improving* the work of their predecessors, in such a way that a Whiggish progression ran from Rowe to Pope to Theobald to Warburton to Johnson and Steevens; Malone, however, obsessively returned to the *authority* of the *authentick texts* (my italics to emphasise his two key terms). Deference to the most venerable established authority was the key to his scholarly procedure. The original quartos and folios of Shakespeare were for Malone what the ancient English constitution was for Burke. Taylor summarises the argument which de Grazia develops in detail: 'In Malone's treatment of Shakespeare, as in Burke's treatment of the French Revolution, what is altogether new is by definition spurious; the past validates; past authority authenticates present actions'.[7]

I do not doubt the truth of this as a reading of Malone. What I do want to question is the view that his appropriation of Shakespeare for anti-revolutionary purposes was hegemonic in the 1790s. I think that *Shakespeare Verbatim* obscures the complexity of what happened to Shakespeare at this time; I am interested in the way that he was *contested*, in the resistance to Malone's juggernaut. It is, I believe, important to insist on Shakespeare's status as a totem who has continually been struggled over, not least because there are struggles ahead of us in matters of curriculum and canon, themselves forms of indirect

[7] *Reinventing Shakespeare*, p. 133.

censorship. The current dispute about what should be taught as
'English' in the National Curriculum often seems to come down to a
battle between 'traditionalists' who stand up for Shakespeare as the
representative of 'our cultural heritage' – 'heritage', that Burkean
concept which is so central to the self-image of post-imperial Britain –
and 'radicals' who appeal to 'relevance', the 'contemporary', the
'multi-cultural', English as communication and media studies rather
than the reverential study of canonical texts. Shakespeare may have
been the flagship of the Traditionalists in the two hundred years since
Malone, but throughout that time there have also been 'alternative
Shakespeares', 'radical' appropriations.

Gary Taylor, it should be acknowledged, does mention one important anti-Malone figure of the 1790s, but he sees him as isolated and
quickly suppressed, not symptomatic of a broader tendency. This was
Joseph Ritson, whose 1792 *Cursory Criticisms on the Edition of
Shakspeare published by Edmond Malone* was to the 1790 edition what
Paine's *Rights of Man* was to Burke's *Reflections*. 'Citizen Ritson', as he
was known, wore his own politics on his sleeve; in the preface to the
Cursory Criticisms, he wondered how the editors of the established
reviews and magazines could get away with their malicious invective
(which they had been directing at him for years), 'while offenders of
comparative insignificance are almost every day exposed on pillories,
or perishing in dungeons'.[8] This is more than an allusion to the
inequality of rich and poor before the law, for at this time any reference to petty offenders perishing in dungeons would have evoked the
storming of the Bastille. Then in the main body of Ritson's attack on
Malone we find the following:

> King Richard, it is well known, had as good a title to the crown as
> the late king William or queen Anne, or the reigning house of
> Hanover. The issue of King Edward had been *bastardized*, the duke
> of Clarence *attainted*, and himself *declared the undoubted heir of
> Richard duke of York*, BY ACT OF PARLIAMENT: and what better title
> has the present king?[9]

Even the typography does political work here, as king, queen, and

[8] Joseph Ritson, *Cursory Criticisms on the Edition of Shakspeare published by
Edmond Malone* (London, 1792), p. v.
[9] *Cursory Criticisms*, p. 77, quoted, Taylor, *Reinventing Shakespeare*, pp.
145–6.

duke are cut down to lower-case. It had been important for Malone that he should deny the right to the throne of the tyrannical Richard III; Ritson, using precisely the technique that Paine had used against Burke – that is to say, stressing the fissures in the English monarchy, the fact that there is no organic royal family tree extending back to 1066 – turns the argument against both the settlement of 1688 and the present king.

Malone's reply to Ritson, also published in 1792, leaves no doubt that the *Cursory Criticisms* were taken politically. Ritson's attack is negligible, Malone implies, since the 1790 edition had, to his great honour and gratification, received wide approbation from the people who really mattered, foremost among whom was 'Mr Burke, whose mind is of such a grasp as to embrace at once the greatest and the minutest objects, and who, in the midst of his numerous and import- ant avocations [i.e. attacking the French Revolution and all its works], has always found time for the calmer pursuits of philosophy and polite literature'.[10] Ritson's pamphlet is condemned as 'vulgar ribaldry' – 'let it rest with the low societies among whom it has been picked up' (p. 4). One could imagine Burke saying exactly the same of Paine's reply to his work. Malone then goes on to describe his own procedures in terms of dependence on the *'authority'* of the 'authen- tick copies', and contempt for the 'capricious innovations' of all later editions from the second folio onwards (pp. 22–3). Such phrases as 'capricious innovations' are the common currency of English anti- jacobinism.

Malone's commanding position among the booksellers allowed him to marginalise Citizen Joseph and effectively censor a Ritson Shakes- peare out of existence. But it was not only Ritson whom he had to see off in the course of the 1790s. I have quoted a letter he received from Burke in 1796 on the subject of Shakespearean scholarship and anti- revolutionary fervour. Its occasion was the publication on 31 March 1796 of Malone's weighty book, *An Inquiry into the Authenticity of Certain Miscellaneous Papers and Legal Instruments, published Dec. 24, 1795 and Attributed to Shakspeare, Queen Elizabeth, and Henry, Earl of Southampton: Illustrated by Fac-Similes of the Genuine Hand-Writing of that Nobleman, and of Her Majesty; a new Fac-simile of the Hand-Writing of Shakspeare, never before Exhibited; And other Authentick Documents: In a Letter Addressed to the Right Hon. James, Earl of Charlemont.* One

---

[10] Malone, *A Letter to the Rev. Richard Farmer* (London, 1792), p. 2.

notes here precisely the apparatus that de Grazia has identified as characteristic of Malone: the concern for authenticity and original documents, some of them actually reproduced in facsimile as forensic evidence, together with the genuflexions towards crown and nobility (Elizabeth as 'Her Majesty', the dressing up of the text as a letter to an aristocratic patron). The object of his attack was the elaborately produced *Miscellaneous Papers and Legal Instruments under the Hand and Seal of William Shakspeare, including the Tragedy of King Lear, and a Small Fragment of Hamlet, from the Original MSS. in the Possession of Samuel Ireland*. Malone's conclusive demonstration that these documents were fakes was well timed because it was published on the eve of the scheduled performance at Drury Lane of the ultimate production from the Ireland document factory, Shakespeare's lost play, *Vortigern, An Historical Tragedy*. J. P. Kemble had planned the première, with himself playing the lead, for April the first, though at the last minute he was persuaded to put it off for a day so as not to seem Foolish. An amazing five hundred copies of Malone's four hundred page book sold on 31st March and 1st April. Unsurprisingly, the performance of *Vortigern* the following day provoked uproar during act five scene two when Kemble pronounced the unfortunate lines

> And with rude laughter, and fantastic tricks,
> Thou clap'st thy rattling fingers to the sides;
> And when this solemn mockery is ended . . .[11]

The Ireland affair was the last and greatest of the eighteenth-century literary forgery scandals. It is a story that has been told a number of times, most wittily by Samuel Schoenbaum in *Shakespeare's Lives*. And it does make a very funny story. How on earth, we wonder, can so many of the literati of the day, from the Poet Laureate and James Boswell downwards, have been taken in by such farragos as 'A Letter from Shakspeare to Anna Hatherrewaye' and 'A Deed of Gift from William Shakspeare to William Henry Ireland', in which Elizabethan spelling was represented as a matter of putting as many double consonants and ees on the ends of words as could possibly be fitted in (e.g. Shakespeare's memorandum to himself appended to his letter from Queen Elizabeth: 'Thys Letterre I dydde receyve fromme mye moste gracyouse Ladye Elizabethe ande I doe requeste itte maye bee kepte

---

11 *Vortigern, An Historical Tragedy, in Five Acts; represented at the Theatre Royal, Drury Lane, on Saturday, April 2, 1796* (London, 1799), p. 64.

withe alle care possyble'[12])? But we should not merely laugh. For all the scholarly advances of the last two hundred years, a very distinguished historian can still authenticate the Hitler Diaries. When you want something badly enough, it is easy to close your eyes.

Boswell knelt down in front of the Ireland documents and pronounced the Nunc Dimittis. Any student of medieval religion can tell you about the manufacture of relics: the forger William Henry Ireland was simply performing a service for true believers in the cult of Shakespeare that had been formalised by Garrick's Jubilee of 1769. He wrote his confession – itself a highly literary thing to do – very soon after Malone's exposure, and in it he claimed that he was only trying to please his father, Samuel Ireland. The latter was an arch-Bardolater, and his son thought that it would make the old man happy to have a document in Shakespeare's hand, so he fabricated one for him. But once it was widely credited, William Henry, 'urged, partly by the world' and partly by his 'own vanity',[13] could not stop himself producing another one – and another, and another, until he eventually got round to some *Hamlet* and *Lear* manuscripts and the complete text of *Vortigern*. Samuel Ireland's motives for publishing the material were presumably primarily financial – hence the expensive format in which the *Miscellaneous Papers and Legal Instruments* was produced – and secondarily associated with reputation (the hope that his family name and his Norfolk Street home would for ever be associated with this greatest of all literary discoveries). Astonishingly, he seems to have continued to believe in the authenticity of the documents even after his son had confessed that they were fabrications.

What becomes of Shakespeare in all this? He is made into a commodity, and in this sense the affair is paradigmatic of eighteenth-century England as a consumer society. Samuel Ireland was an archetypal entrepreneur in that he began from low origins as a weaver, but then made his money as a printseller. He was a beneficiary of the economic expansion whereby more and more people had the leisure and the money to purchase prints and books. Forgery was a threat in the eighteenth-century cultural marketplace for the same reason that the counterfeiting of coin and paper money is a threat to the economy

---

[12] Quoted, Malone, *An Inquiry into the Authenticity of Certain Miscellaneous Papers and Legal Instruments* (London, 1796), p. 26.
[13] W. H. Ireland, *An Authentic Account of the Shaksperian Manuscripts, &c.* (London, 1796), p. 9.

of any such society. William Dodd, we should remember, has two
claims to fame: his *Beauties of Shakespear*, a hugely successful anthology of purple passages that made Shakespeare available to a much
wider audience than ever before (the *Reader's Digest* principle), and
his unhappy end, hanged as a counterfeiter after forging the signature
of his former pupil, Lord Chesterfield, on a bond for over four thousand pounds. The 1709 Copyright Act made literature into property;
thereafter, forgery was the capital literary crime (the reasons why
plagiarism took over from forgery as the most heinous crime in the age
of Coleridge are complex and fascinating, but they are not my subject
here). The Ireland affair, then, was very much of its age – it had its
forebears in the controversies surrounding Macpherson's Ossian,
Chatterton's Rowley, and especially Lauder's Milton.

Essentially, then, Malone was troubled by the forgeries and needed
to cut them down because they debased the cultural coinage. And
since in the 1790s he was motivated by his Burkean anti-revolution-
ism to use the cultural heritage, embodied in Shakespeare, as a means
of shoring up the nation, the Ireland papers presented a political
threat. These texts were precisely the kind of 'capricious innovations'
that he had set out to eradicate; they undermined the textual Authorities he had so carefully marshalled in his 1790 edition. The *Inquiry*
was a detection of literary impostures, and as such it recommended
itself to Burke as a parallel to his own detections of political impostures (i.e. Jacobinism). In the covering letter with the complimentary
copy he sent to Burke on 1 April 1796, Malone proudly proclaimed
himself a brother-in-arms: 'As for my political principles, which I
have more than once introduced, I expect to be attacked for them by
those who are in the pay of the French Regicides and by Messrs
Thellwall and Co – but why should you have that honour all to
yourself?'[14]

On page two of his *Inquiry* Malone openly asserted his patriotism by
saying that the English have a right to boast of Shakespeare and that,
accordingly, 'proportionate to our respect and veneration for that
extraordinary man ought to be our care of his fame, and of those
valuable writings that he has left us; and our solicitude to preserve
them pure and unpolluted by any modern sophistication or foreign
admixture whatsoever'. The language here is marked by a strong sense
of national cultural identity; the last phrase is manifestly a gibe at

[14] *Correspondence of Burke*, VIII, 454.

French innovation. 'I am the more anxious to seize the present moment,' Malone continues, 'because, in this interval of the political warfare, the cause of Shakspeare and the Muses has a chance to be heard' (p. 3). Ostensibly, the Ireland affair is addressed as a relief from politics, but the conjunction of the two causes in the same sentence suggests that the argument will be an extension of the political warfare by other means.

Ireland's 'Letter from Shakspeare to Anna Hatherrewaye' included two phrases that Malone found especially objectionable: 'I praye you perfume thys mye poore Locke with thye balmye kysses forre thenne indeede shalle Kynges themmselves bowe ande paye homage toe itte' and 'Neytherre the gyldedde bawble thatte envyrrones the heade of Majestye noe norre honourres moste weyghtye wulde give mee halfe the joye as didde thysse mye lyttle worke forre thee'.[15] William Henry Ireland later claimed that he merely used these images because he wanted to suggest that Shakespeare really did love his wife, but Malone put a very different construction on them:

> from the present contemptuous mention of KINGS, it is no very wild conjecture to suppose that the unknown writer is not extremely adverse to those modern republican zealots who have for some time past employed their feeble, but unwearied, endeavours to diminish that love and veneration which every true Briton feels, and I trust will ever feel, for ROYALTY, so happily and beneficially inwoven in our estimable constitution. Such, however, was his ignorance of the period to which the Letter before us must be referred, that, for the sake of the sentiment, the contemptuous language of the present day is introduced at a time when it was as little known, as the orthography and phraseology which the writer has employed. (pp. 148–9)

The opportunity is then taken to introduce a paean to Elizabeth I and a fierce attack on 'The detestable doctrines of French Philosophy and the imaginary Rights of Man'; the Elizabethan period is made into a golden age of degree and of reverence for those in authority, 'from the *worshipful* Justice of the Peace to the grave counsellors and splendid courtiers who surrounded the throne' (p. 151). The vision is of the organic England praised so eloquently by Burke. One might pause

---

[15] Quoted, *Inquiry*, pp. 144, 148.

here to consider Shakespeare's representation of courtiers and Justices of the Peace. Are Shallow and Silence really exemplary lawgivers?

Malone must have assumed that they were, for his Shakespeare had a 'tender mind' which was incapable of criticising the established order of things. The youthful Bard, we are informed, was 'impressed with a sense of loyalty' from his lessons in the schoolroom and from the Homilies against disobedience and rebellion which he heard in church. In the forged letter, on the other hand, he 'is made to express himself concerning the diadem of kings, in the style which one of the Regicides would have used in the following century, or one of the Rulers of France would employ at this day' (p. 154). The link between the regicide of 1649 and that of 1793 is a move typical of the anti-jacobin rhetoric of the 1790s. Malone goes on to argue that Shakespeare always viewed the crown as being made of true gold, not superficially gilded – the sub-text here is that the dramatist believed in the sacredness of the crown and did not regard it in terms of mere surface gloss, of empty show. A further attempt is made to nail the idea of an anti-regal Shakespeare by means of the argument that the word 'bauble' was not used to mean 'crown' in the sixteenth century. Malone's motivation in this was, I suggest, a recognition that to call the crown a gilded bauble was to demystify it, to make it into a flimsy metaphor in precisely the way that Paine had done in a famous passage of the *Rights of Man*. Under the new French constitution, Paine pointed out, the right of war and peace resided in the nation because it was the nation which paid the expense, but

> In England, this right is said to reside in a *metaphor*, shown at the Tower for sixpence or a shilling apiece: So are the lions; and it would be a step nearer to reason to say it resided in them, for any inanimate metaphor is not more than a hat or a cap. We can all see the absurdity of worshipping Aaron's molten calf, or Nebuchadnezzar's golden image; but why do men continue to practise themselves the absurdities they despise in others?[16]

In the partisan discourse of the 1790s, when so many words carried political weight, William Ireland's fancy of Shakespeare writing to his love about a bauble took on unexpected importance. To crown his examination of the mischievous word, Malone proceeded to quote a

---

[16] Thomas Paine, *Rights of Man* (1791–2, repr. Harmondsworth, 1969), p. 99.

series of passages in support of the view that Shakespeare subscribed unquestioningly to the doctrine of the divine right of kings. The slightest possibility of a Painite as opposed to a Burkean reading of the plays is quashed.

In his peroration, Malone claimed that previous forgeries, such as those of Ossian and Rowley, were 'harmless and innocent compared with the present fabrication, whether it be considered with a view to society, or to the character and history of the incomparable poet whose handwriting has been counterfeited' (p. 352). The undermining of Shakespeare, he implies, is the undermining of England; Ireland's inept forgeries are nothing less than a threat to society. 'Johnson! thou should'st be living at this hour' is the thrust of Malone's final response to the threat: if that great Cham of literature had still been alive, he would have animadverted more effectively than anyone else against, first, republicanism and French principles, and second, the forgeries. Malone actually reproduces the letter of confession which Johnson wrote for Lauder as a recantation of the forgery-based claim that Milton was a plagiarist, substituting Shakespeare's name for Milton, and inviting the Irelands to sign it. Finally, a dream is recorded in which Malone is Shakespeare's legal Counsel in Parnassus; he pleads his case, and Apollo pronounces sentence in the literary property suit – 'the rights of authors were as sacred as any other'; the 1709 Copyright Act 'guarded their literary property from every kind of invasion' and it should be extended to take into account a case like the one in question, where the injury is done long after the author is dead (p. 360). A 'hue and cry' is made after the contrivers of the fabrication and Apollo further orders the burning of all surviving copies of the *Miscellaneous Papers and Legal Instruments*, to be carried out by a kind of scholarly Committee of Public Safety consisting of Farmer, Steevens, Tyrwhitt and Malone himself (p. 361).

The close of the *Inquiry* is a late contribution to the long eighteenth-century copyright argument, which was so intimately bound up with the making of literature into a commodity, with the ownership and merchandising of texts. But Malone's notions of 'invasion' and the attack on 'property' also impinge on the revolution debate. And the words of Apollo as he passes sentence carry some harsh overtones: the years from 1794 onwards were marked by 'hue and cry' against potential traitors (not so long after Malone wrote the *Inquiry*, let us remember, the government agent James Walsh was despatched to Alfoxden and heard talk of Spy Nozy), while the proscribing of the book echoes Pitt's Act of 1795 suppressing seditious publications.

Why such strong stuff? It is partly accounted for by Malone's particular obsession with authenticity and authority, his hatred of capricious innovation. Forgery is the ultimate sedition against literary authority. But I suspect that Malone was also driven by a sense that oppositional forces were getting their hands on Shakespeare. In a letter of December 1795 he referred to Samuel Ireland as 'a broken Spitalfields weaver'.[17] One could not have weavers repossessing the National Bard. It is interesting in this regard that the radical Ritson was one of the first people to examine and see through the forgeries; he made quite clear in private letters that he was not taken in by them for a moment, but he said nothing in print on the subject – might this have been out of a certain sympathy for Ireland as a fellow-outsider, another non-establishment Shakespearean? I certainly think it is significant that the Certificate of Belief signed by public figures who accepted the documents as genuine was instigated by Samuel Parr, the great Whig and friend of Priestley and other radicals. Parr's name at the top of the list of true believers definitively marked the Ireland camp out as oppositional; the declaration was also signed by a number of other prominent anti-Pitt activists, such as the Earl of Lauderdale. When a public debate on the forgeries was announced for 9 January 1797, the notice advertising it stated that no political remarks would be permitted in the discussion – presumably this statement was necessary because the issue was perceived as a political one by this time, and there was a probability that such remarks would be made.

Samuel Ireland's own reply to Malone, *Mr Ireland's Vindication of his Conduct, respecting the publication of the supposed Shakspeare Manuscripts*, appeared in November 1796, *after* his son's confession. It took the form of a plea for free speech: 'The most unequivocal characteristic of an enlightened age, is the licence which is indulged to all, of free communication with the public on doubtful, and controverted subjects' (p. 1). About a year later, Ireland published a second reply, accusing Malone of policing the Bard, desiring to appropriate Shakespeare exclusively for himself, imagining 'that the very name of Shakspeare is not to be pronounced without his licence or indulgence'.[18] With considerable penetration, Ireland exposes Malone's ideological motivation. The influence on the *Inquiry* of the author's own 'political tenets' is pointed out: 'to shew a seditious tendency in some

---

[17] Quoted, Samuel Schoenbaum, *Shakespeare's Lives* (Oxford, 1970), p. 232.
[18] Samuel Ireland, *An Investigation of Mr Malone's Claim to the Character of Scholar, or Critic* (London, 1797 or 1798), p. 7.

passages of the manuscripts would excite a powerful, and efficient prejudice against them.' 'For this purpose,' Ireland continues, Malone 'introduces himself as a zealous royalist' and 'imputes a seditious construction' to the passage from the supposed letter to Anna Hatherrewaye (p. 81). Malone's extracts demonstrating Shakespeare's loyalty are then challenged with others from the plays that call the crown something very like a gilded bauble; Ireland thus counters the image of the loyal Bard with that of a dramatist capable of exposing 'the emptiness of royalty' (p. 82). He also questions Malone's idealisation of Elizabeth's rule, arguing that such a construction was part of a wider – and politically motivated – tendency in the 1790s to view her reign as a golden age, while in fact it was a time when 'the liberties of the people' were overlooked or despised:

> Mr Malone in his abhorrence of regicide, ought not to have forgot the cruel murder of the Scottish Queen, in which a lawful and amiable sovereign was deposed by the artful, and jealous policy of the princess, of whom he is so violently enamoured. (pp. 83–4)

(It might be noted in passing here that another text of 1796 was the *Observations on Hamlet* of James Plumptre, which argued that the play may have contained veiled allusions to the murder of Mary Queen of Scots.)

In Ireland's view, Malone admired the Elizabethan age because it was a time of British success in war and prosperity in commerce – because, that is, it was a model of the Britain he would have liked to see again. What Malone suppressed was that it was also a period during which government was 'uniformly conducted on the most arbitrary, and tyrannical principles' (p. 84). In response to Malone's argument that Shakespeare could not have written the 'gilded bauble' passage because he was a loyalist, Ireland makes the very legitimate point that of course you can find loyalist passages in Shakespeare, spoken by kings, bishops, and courtiers, but that this loyalism is what is only natural in the mouths of such characters; it belongs to them and does not necessarily represent Shakespeare's own political outlook. Since his form is dramatic, Shakespeare can put forward a plurality of political positions:

> Hence it is, that in the writings of Shakspeare, it is easy to select passages, in which the most servile, and submissive principles are inculcated. But on the other hand, it is by no means difficult to find

sentiments, which breathe the spirit of a proud and dignified independence. (p. 87)

The republican play of *Julius Caesar* is especially singled out as a
repository of the latter kind of sentiment.

Ireland undoubtedly has the better of these arguments. His reading
of the Elizabethan age is more recognizable to us than is the Merrie
England invented by Malone; his awareness of the ease of selectivity
and hence partiality in the attempt to adduce Shakespeare's politics
from his plays reveals him as a pioneer in the analysis of criticism as
an ideologically-loaded activity, of the way in which readings of texts
are shaped by the reader's own predilections. To demonstrate the
plurality of possible political appropriations of Shakespeare was to
break up the hegemony which Malone had been seeking to establish.

Conveniently for those like Malone who wanted a monolithic and
conservative Shakespeare, Ireland could be ridiculed for his continued belief in the documents and pilloried for his greed in putting
them on the market in lavish folio at four guineas a copy to sub-
scribers. His iconoclastic argument about the partisan nature of interpretation could thus be ignored. But the same argument also came
from another, more respectable quarter. George Chalmers had an
unimpeachable pedigree as a lawyer, a scholarly if pedantic antiquary,
and a minor government official working under Lord Liverpool. He
was also a fully paid-up Burkean, insofar as he had written a scathing
Life of Thomas Pain, With a Defence of his Writings, which was in fact
an uncompromising attack on his writings. In 1796, however, in
response to the prosecution of his colleague, John Reeves, for seditious libel over his *Thoughts on the English Government*, he published
an anonymous *Vindication of the Privilege of the People in respect of the
Constitutional Right of Free Discussion*. Chalmers was a virulent anti-
Jacobin, but in order to defend Reeves's right to publish his extreme
anti-democratic opinions, he was forced to concede the principle of
free speech and thus implicitly accept the right to publish of Paine,
Thelwall, and the other English Jacobins. Ironically enough, the
Chalmers who had gone into print against the *Rights of Man* found
himself cast in the role of Paine to Malone's Burke.

Taken in by the Ireland forgeries and then provoked by the lofty,
authoritarian tone of Malone's *Inquiry*, Chalmers proceeded to yoke
his newfound sense of the importance of free speech with his antiquarian interests, and in 1797 he published a six hundred and twenty-
eight page *Apology for the Believers in the Shakspeare-Papers*, following

it two years later with a six hundred and fifty-four page *Supplemental Apology . . . being a reply to Mr Malone's Answer, which was early announced, but never published*. All these replies and counter-replies and replies to replies that were not actually written suggest a polemical pattern that replicates the debate on the French Revolution which, thanks to the opening shots of Burke and Paine, so dominated the printing-presses throughout the 1790s.

Chalmers acknowledged from the outset that the Ireland documents were forgeries, but argued that Malone's *Inquiry* was an attempt to stifle free speech and public debate. He referred to Malone throughout as 'the public accuser', making him sound like the kind of man who would stand up in the Convention in Paris and unleash a public denunciation dispatching some hapless rival to the guillotine. If Malone and Pitt have their way, Chalmers seems to be saying, the liberality and plurality allowed for by the flexible British constitution will be lost. Chalmers works with the language of the law which he knew so well:

> I will proceed, if this court will grant me its indulgent attention, and favour me with its accustomed patience, to show cause why an information should not be filed against those believers, who, claiming the right of fair discussion, and of free exemption from the authority of a dictator, within the republic of letters, are ambitious of appearing in this enlightened presence, without being deem'd 'some untutor'd youths, unskilful in the world's false forgeries.'[19]

The loading here is in favour of 'rights' and against 'authority'; the realm of letters is imagined as a 'republic', not an 'aristocracy', as it was for Burke and Malone. The opponent of revolution is suddenly speaking the language of the revolutionaries.

Chalmers had the material to match Malone point for point in historical scholarship, and he succeeded in creating a very different image of Elizabethan England. Where Malone had said that the 'contemptuous' modern anti-monarchical language of the letter to Anna Hatherrewaye was anachronistic, Chalmers quietly pointed to the works of George Buchanan – his *De Jure* 'contained the seed-plot of the French principles of the present day' (*Apology*, p. 184). Where Malone had blithely asserted of the Queen that 'she unquestionably

---

[19] George Chalmers, *An Apology for the Believers in the Shakspeare-Papers* (London, 1797), p. 2.

was not in that age thought to infringe the liberties of the people' (*Inquiry*, p. 150), Chalmers advanced evidence to the contrary, drawing attention to puritan sermons and pamphlets that were proclaimed to be traitorous. That there were '*free principles*' and '*free practices*' – the terms again have contemporary French overtones – in the sixteenth century is demonstrable, Chalmers suggests, from the passing of the 1589 Licensing Act which prevented the players from handling 'certen matters of *divinytie*, and of *state* unfitt to be suffered' (*Apology*, p. 186n.). You do not need a censorship if there is not sedition in the air: 'The privy-council did not so much partake of the scenic enthusiasm of the people, as they viewed the popular concourse to scenic representations, in the light of a political disorder; which, having increased under restraint, required correction, rather than countenance' (p. 410). The apparent orthodoxy of Shakespeare's plays is attributable to the censorship, not to the dramatist's natural loyalty.

Chalmers laid particular emphasis on the Essex plot, dwelling on the involvement in it of Shakespeare's patron, the Earl of Southampton. The association with Southampton and the performance of *Richard II* commissioned by the rebels on the eve of their rebellion are invoked to make a tacit link between Shakespeare and the Essex faction. Putative Essex allusions are found in the plays: in *Richard II*, Shakespeare 'laid his satirical finger upon the weak, temporizing, shifting, policy of Elizabeth, which gave every possible encouragement to the rebels'; *Timon of Athens* 'is an accurate delineation of the state of men, and things, in London, during the year 1601, and the existence of Essex's rebellion'.[20] This Shakespeare is no fawning sycophant of majesty.

Given that he was such an anti-Painite, there is an astonishingly strong vein of populism in Chalmers's version of Shakespeare. One of the main planks of Malone's case had been the argument that the forgeries used words which did not exist in the sixteenth century. Chalmers replies that language belongs to the people and does not only exist in books – that Malone could not find a word in the tomes in his library did not necessarily mean that it did not exist. Shakespeare, it is concluded in the *Apology*, got more 'popular applause' than 'distinguished patronage' (p. 599). A Shakespeare whose rapport was with the people more than the patrons was a very

---

[20] Chalmers, *A Supplemental Apology for the Believers in the Shakspeare-Papers* (London, 1799), pp. 309, 391.

different beast from the character carefully domesticated by Malone in his 1790 biography.

Gary Taylor argues that the Romantic emphasis on character, on Shakespearean drama as a matter of individual psychology, was part of the conservative appropriation of the Bard:

> Coleridge's interpretation of Hamlet distanced and idealized the political irresolution of his own generation. Coleridge projected that collective indecision into Hamlet and then made an artistic fetish of his own weakness . . . he made 'doing nothing' seem Shakespearian, heroic, and tragic.[21]

But Chalmers advanced a different way of reading Shakespearean tragedy, one that began with society rather than the exquisitely sensitive but paralysed individual consciousness. There was famine in England in 1608–9, the period in which Shakespeare wrote *Coriolanus*, and, according to Chalmers, in that play 'The tragedy turns upon the *existing dearth*'.[22] The phrasing here is decisive: the play does not merely allude to contemporary events, the tragedy *turns upon* social conditions. Buried within the Ireland controversy and emanating from the pen of a writer who elsewhere reveals himself to be an arch-conservative, we find an approach to Shakespearean drama that is more Brechtian than Coleridgean. Gary Taylor is right that Shakespeare is always being reinvented. But in periods like the 1790s he was remade in much more varied ways than Taylor thinks. William Henry Ireland's extreme reinvention by means of forgery was of course doomed, but it had the important effect of keeping Shakespeare controversial and ensuring his continuing afterlife in camps other than that of Burke and Malone.

There is also a more general conclusion to be drawn from the case. In his book *Forgers and Critics*, Anthony Grafton shows, principally by means of examples from the Renaissance, that there is a curious symbiosis between literary forgery and authentic scholarship – historical criticism 'has been dependent for its development on the stimulus that forgers have provided'.[23] The Ireland affair certainly bears this argument out, in that the forgeries provoked significant scholarly research from Malone and Chalmers. It is, however, possible to go

---

21 *Reinventing Shakespeare*, p. 102.

22 *Supplemental Apology*, p. 436.

23 Grafton, *Forgers and Critics: Creativity and Duplicity in Western Scholarship* (Princeton, 1990), p. 123.

further than Grafton, who ultimately denies that forgery and historical criticism are in any sense identical, for what the defences by
Ireland and Chalmers reveal is that the exposure of a supposed text
from the past as fiction is dependent on the creation of an alternative
image of the past, which in its own way is also a fiction, in that it is
the product of a present need. The defenders of the right to forge
show that Malone read Shakespeare selectively in order to make him
look like Burke, and in that sense it was Malone who forged him
anew. It is not a coincidence that the key word is ambiguous: both the
fabricator and the supposedly disinterested scholar were in fact in the
business of *forging their own cultural identity*. And in a decade as ideo-
logically riven as the 1790s, that identity was perforce political.
Faking it revealed that Malone's re-making of it was a form of
censorship.

'Examples of Safe Printing': Censorship and Popular Radical Literature in the 1790s

JON MEE

THE 1790s have been described by Alfred Cobban as the decade which witnessed 'perhaps the last real discussion of the fundamentals of politics' in Britain. There is an important sense in which the literature produced by the controversy over the French Revolution can be seen as a 'discussion' of principles. Yet the term 'discussion' suggests a polite exchange of views in a liberal public sphere, a picture which seems very distant from the experience of most of those who participated at the popular end of the struggle over political change in the 1790s. From the Royal Proclamation of May 1792 against seditious writing onwards, it was apparent to radical writers that they could not simply express their desire for change directly without facing the threat of prosecution. Those who wished to continue to have their say were forced to consider new ways of challenging the status quo among which were a variety of rhetorical strategies of indirection.[1]

The rhetoric of 'philosophical radicalism' has been the focus of a recent article by John Barrell.[2] His main emphasis is on the treason trials of 1794 which saw David Downie and Robert Watt found guilty

---

[1] See Cobban, *The Debate on the French Revolution, 1789–1800* (London, 1950), p. 31. My point about the inadequacy of the term 'discussion' is far from original. See also Marilyn Butler, *Burke, Paine, Godwin and the Revolution Controversy* (Cambridge, 1984), pp. 1–2, and Mark Philp, 'Introduction' pp. 1–17 (pp. 1–2) and 'The Fragmentary Ideology of Reform', pp. 50–77 (p. 61), in *The French Revolution and British Popular Politics*, ed. Philp (Cambridge, 1991).

[2] John Barrell, 'Imaginary Treason, Imaginary Law: The State Trials of 1794' in *The Birth of Pandora and the Division of Knowledge* (London, 1992), pp. 119–143. Barrell seems to accept the term 'philosophical radicalism' as fairly unproblematically indicating a discourse of enlightenment rationalism close to Godwin's philosophy and Horne Tooke's theories of language. Although this category does seem to nominate an important strand of radical discourse, it scarcely ever exists as a pristine ideology (not even in Godwin's writing) in any particular text.

in Edinburgh and Thomas Hardy, John Horne Tooke, and John Thelwall acquitted in London. Barrell's object is to dramatise the 'conflict between the various discourses in which politics was debated in that decade' (p. 119). At the same time his essay is also an explicit intervention in contemporary debates in literary theory. Barrell wants to use the treason trials to show that 'we may need to be wary of assuming an easy opposition between mobility and fixity, and of attributing a progressive character to what unfixes, loosens, undermines the authority of logos' and a 'reactionary character to whatever valorises the fixity of language' (p. 120). Specifically in relation to the treason trials, Barrell seeks to show that 'it is because the defence believes so firmly in the authority of logos that it is able to mock the pretended stability of the language of law, and to reveal its actual instability' (p. 120).

Barrell's claim that it is the historical specificity of an act of writing which must determine whether a particular instance of rhetorical indeterminacy is to be judged as progressive or not is surely correct. But what I want to suggest is that Barrell's concentration on the treason trials and what he calls 'philosophical radicalism' has lead him to a rather narrow version of the very historical specificity with which he engages. The controversy which raged in Britain around the French Revolution in the 1790s witnessed a remarkable efflorescence of popular radical literature. This literature needs to be distinguished from the philosophical radicalism which is Barrell's concern and, indeed, which has always dominated literary investigations into the radicalism of the decade. Far from participating in any Englightenment dream of a fixed, transparent language, much popular radical literature delighted in linguistic evasiveness. It did so, I would argue, for a variety of specific historical reasons, not the least of which were the conditions of censorship under which such publications had to operate in the 1790s. It is the relationship between popular radical literature and the conditions of censorship on which I shall concentrate in this essay.[3]

---

[3] Iain McCalman has made a useful distinction between 'respectable' and 'unrespectable' culture within popular radicalism itself in *Radical Underworld: Prophets, Revolutionaries, and Pornographers in London, 1795–1840* (Cambridge, 1988), especially pp. 26–34. The focus of this article might be said to be on the latter, although again particular individuals and texts, as McCalman himself demonstrates, cannot be simply assigned to one category or another without distorting the fluidity and complexity of the culture of the 1790s.

1. *What were the conditions of censorship in the 1790s?*

Men and women of radical convictions believed that they were wit-nessing a reign of terror in the 1790s. Whether the means of coercion applied by the government really amounted to a Terror remains a subject of debate among historians.[4] In part the difficulty in assessing the extent to which radicalism was repressed has its origins in the variety of the forms of coercion available. Apart from the explicitly political prosecutions which provide the focus for this article, Pitt and the government often employed informal means which did not necessarily lead to court appearances. Publishers could be pressured through their creditors, for instance, and the debtor's prison could be used as a place to keep radicals out of circulation. John Reeves's Association for the Protection of Liberty and Property against Repub-licans and Levellers played an important part in the repression of radical opinion. The organization had no official government support, but members of the government were involved in a personal capacity in its origins and it is likely that funding was received from the government. The Association was able to threaten and intimidate radical activists in a range of informal ways such as putting pressure on their employers and 'advising' publicans not to rent their rooms for radical debating societies. While not amounting to official censorship as such, the activities of the Association fed into the chief legal means by which radical writing was controlled – the law of seditious libel – since it was individual magistrates (many of them members of the Association), ordinary individuals, or groups like the Reeves association, who had to bring a person to trial and finance the pro-ceedings. Perhaps compared with what was happening in France at the time this is very far from Terror, but it was also a context which made it difficult for radicals to continue to believe in the boasted liberties of Englishmen.[5]

---

4 See Clive Emsley, 'Repression, "terror" and the rule of law in England during the decade of the French Revolution', *English Historical Review* (1985), 801–827 and 'An aspect of Pitt's "Terror": prosecutions for sedition during the 1790s', *Social History* 6 (1981), 155–84. Emsley's view of the range of coercive practices pursued by the government is rather narrow. See Mark Philp's comments, 'Fragmentary Ideology of Reform', pp. 62–3.
5 On Pitt's use of bankruptcy and other forms of covert pressure, see L. Werkmeister, *A Newspaper History of England, 1792–1793* (Lincoln, Neb., 1967), pp. 228–38 and 345. An interesting case in point is the elaborate

Clive Emsley has shown that most of the overtly political trials in the decade involved prosecutions for publishing seditious libels or uttering seditious words.[6] The Court of King's Bench had seen an average of over two prosecutions a year for political libels in the eighteenth century prior to the French Revolution. In the decade after 1789 there were on average over ten a year.[7] Most of these prosecutions came in the earlier part of the decade and were part of the campaign to staunch the flow of literature, stimulated by the publication of Paine's *Rights of Man*, intended to appeal to a popular readership. These prosecutions were not the result of new legislation. The law of seditious libel had been the main means of prosecuting political publications since the demise of statutory licensing at the end of the seventeenth century.[8] The passing into law of Fox's Libel Act in 1792 (32 Geo. III c. 60) had refined and clarified the law in ways that are important to the interests of this article. Before Fox's act it had been unclear whether the magistrate or the jury were to decide if content was libellous. Supporters of the government typically argued that the jury had only to decide on the fact of publication. But this interpretation of the law was repeatedly challenged in the debate over the freedom of the press in the half century preceding Fox's act. The 1792 reform of the statute made it clear that the jury had a right to bring in a verdict of not guilty if they believed the material was not libellous, regardless of the fact of publication. The chances of acquittal were improved by this change because the question of interpretation became a matter for the jury, although evidence suggests that Fox's act did not necessarily lead to more acquittals.

---

strategy Pitt employed to take Sampson Perry, the editor of the *Argus*, out of circulation. See Werkmeister, p. 32.

[6] See 'An aspect of Pitt's Terror', p. 157.

[7] These figures are quoted from Michael Lobban's 'From Seditious Libel to Unlawful Assembly', *Oxford Journal of Legal Studies*, 10 (1990), 309. I am extremely grateful to Dr Lobban for the help he has provided on the legal aspects of this article. Any misunderstandings obviously remain my responsibility.

[8] For a full account of the emergence of seditious libel as the main means of controlling the press 'after other means of restraining the press, such as licensing and treason, became unusable in the mid-1690s', see Philip Hamburger, 'The Development of the Law of Seditious Libel and the Control of the Press', *Stanford Law Review* 37 (1985), 661–765. Also of use is Thomas Andrew Green, *Verdict According to Conscience: Perspectives on the English Criminal Trial Jury 1200–1800* (Chicago, 1985), especially pp. 318–55.

Fox and other critics of the government clearly believed that the change in the law would benefit the liberty of the press. The covert means which Pitt employed to control radical opinion, together with his suspension of habeas corpus from 1794 and the introduction of the so-called 'gagging' acts of 1795, are perhaps indications of the difficulties the government had with using seditious libel as a means of controlling radical opinion. I shall foreground just one of the problems for the government in using seditious libel as a weapon of censorship once the jury's involvement in matters of judgement and degree increased. The procedure of prosecution for seditious libel insisted that the indictment include exact statements of the libels being prosecuted.[9] February 1793 saw Thomas Spence acquitted of selling Paine's *Rights of Man* because the book was misquoted in the bill of indictment. If seemingly insignificant slips of this nature could result in an acquittal, more deeply problematic for the prosecution were those texts where the libel depended on an interpretation of figurative or ironic material. In cases such as these, the prosecution had to specify exactly what the construction was which they put on the words in question. They had to supply a strictly determinate meaning equivalent to the author's intention. The glosses or 'innuendoes' that appear on bills of indictment from the time are not merely explanatory but legal necessities. If it could be shown not simply that the prosecution's interpretation was wrong but that the text was open to other interpretations than the innuendoes provided then the jury had grounds to find the defendant not guilty. What might seem a legal technicality had important consequences for the development of popular radical literature.

Scholars working in the early modern period have recognised the role of conditions of censorship in producing certain kinds of literary practice. The same 'functional ambiguity' which Annabel Patterson, for instance, has traced in the writing of the sixteenth and seventeenth centuries is operative in the 1790s.[10] Radicals inherited a tradition of linguistic indirection which the changes in the seditious libel

---

[9] Michael Lobban has shown that the important judgement about this issue was Lord Chief Justice De Grey's after Horne's trial in 1777. De Grey ruled that in simple libels the meaning ascribed to the libel need not be elaborated but that if the supposed libel were allusive or ironical then the record had to show the imputed meaning. See 'From Seditious Libel', p. 315.

[10] See Patterson, *Censorship and Interpretation: The Conditions of Writing and Reading in Early Modern England* (Madison, Wis., 1984), p. 18.

law of 1792 reinforced. Rather than aspiring to a transparent language of rational debate (the apparent aspiration of many of Barrell's philosophical radicals), an important if neglected section of the literature of the Revolution controversy coveted forms that were both allusive and elusive. The slipperiness of the language was exploited to frustrate the prosecution's legal need to fix determinate meanings on a libel. What I want to do now is exemplify this discussion of the circumstances of radical literature in the 1790s in relation to one particular text, the fable of 'King Chaunticlere' published by Daniel Isaac Eaton in his *Politics for the People* (1793–5).[11]

2. Eaton and 'King Chaunticlere'

Daniel Eaton was one of the most important radical writers and publishers active in the 1790s. He was arrested six times between 1792 and 1795 without being successfully prosecuted. He was finally convicted of seditious libel in 1796, but fled to America. He returned in 1803 and, although he died in 1814 too soon to see what E.P. Thompson has called 'the heroic age of popular Radicalism', his activities on his return are an important link between the 1790s and the later period.[12]

Eaton's *Politics for the People* (1793–5), alternatively titled *Hog's Wash, or a Salmagundy for Swine*, was a deliberate attempt to create a radical literature for the masses in the wake of Paine's *Rights of Man*. Marilyn Butler has pointed out that its intention was 'to challenge Burke's assumptions about the stupidity and non-intellectuality of the masses, by offering them classic texts on politics and commentaries on public affairs', though along with this challenge went a delight in putting texts from the high culture, such as Lord Chesterfield's letters to his son, to 'low' transgressive ends.[13] In addition to these classics were included a more traditionally popular sort of text, including allegories and fables such as 'King Chaunticlere'. This particular fable like many others may not have been written by Eaton himself but culled from other sources (Eaton claimed that it originated with John

11 Eaton published 'King Chaunticlere' in *Politics for the People or Hog's Wash* vol. 1, Pt. 1, no. viii, pp. 102–7.
12 See Thompson, *The Making of the English Working Class*, revised edition (Harmondsworth, 1968), p. 660.
13 Butler, *Burke, Paine, Godwin and the Revolution Controversy*, p. 185.

Thelwall). It is the very unoriginality of 'King Chaunticlere' which interests me, since I believe the rhetoric of the fable is paradigmatic of the strategies of popular radical literature.

The fable, after a lengthy preamble, tells the story of a game cock:

> a haughty sanguinary tyrant, nursed in blood and slaughter from his infancy – fond of foreign wars and domestic rebellions, into which he would sometimes drive his subjects, by his oppressive obstinacy, in hopes that he might increase his power and glory by their suppression. (p. 104)

As the story develops, the topicality of the narrative emerges. The fable quickly, for instance, locks into several of the tropes which Burke's *Reflections* and Paine's answer in *Rights of Man* released into political discourse in the decade. Paine's comment that Burke's elegy for the French monarch and his family 'pities the plumage but forgets the dying bird' is invoked by the following passage (and, in fact, the fable in its entirety):

> Now, though there were some aristocratic prejudices hanging about me, from my education, so that I could not help looking, with considerable reverence, upon the majestic decorations of the person of king Chaunticlere – such as his ermine spotted breast, the fine gold trappings about his neck and shoulders, the flowing robe of plumage tucked up at his rump, and above all, that fine ornamented thing upon his head there – (his crown, or coxcomb, I believe you call it – however the distinction is not very important) – yet I had even at that time some lurking principles of aversion to barefaced despotism, struggling at my heart, which would sometimes whisper to me, that the best things one could do, either for cocks and hens, or men and women, was to rid the world of tyrants. (pp. 104–5)

What is sketched in this passage is a move from a Burkeian respect for the trappings of the ancien regime to a Painite hatred of tyrants, a shift which the fable is presumably intended to induce in its readers.[14]

Apart from the mention of 'plumage', the banter about the crown, 'his crown or coxcomb, I believe you call it', also signals a debt to Paine who never ceases to wrangle about 'what is called the crown' (p. 229) in *Rights of Man*. Indeed one of the passages indicted at Paine's

14 See Paine, *Rights of Man* (Harmondsworth, 1969), p. 51.

trial for seditious libel contained a typical ironic quibble about the word:

> An heretable crown, or an heretable throne, or by what other fanciful name such things may be called, have no other significant explanation than that mankind are heretable property. (p. 172)

Part of Erskine's defence of Paine revolved around the exact signification of the word 'crown' in this passage:

> The sentence, therefore, must either be taken in the pure abstract, and then it is not only merely speculative, but the application of it to our own government fails altogether, or it must be taken connected with the matter which constitutes the application, and then it is MR BURKE'S KING OF ENGLAND, and NOT his Majesty, whose title is denied.

Paine, of course, was found guilty in his absence, but it may be that Erskine's defence highlighted the possibilities available in language to those radicals who sought to take up the challenge thrown out by *Rights of Man*.[15]

The fable of King Chaunticlere is careful to keep the exact referent of its discussion of the crown uncertain. When its narrator says 'if guillotines had been in fashion, I should have certainly guillotined him' the topical nature of what is going on is signalled by the guillotine, but its exact reference is not. Indeed when the fable speaks of 'dragging him immediately to the block' the reader might be reminded of the English example or regicide which preceded Louis XVI's execution – the execution of Charles I – rather than the topical French context. The text does not limit its sphere of allusion only to British history, nor to recent events in France, nor to the prospects back in the Britain of 1794. By keeping its meaning indeterminate, it achieves a critical demystification of monarchy while achieving relative security against prosecution. Moreover it may be that behind the security of the fabular form, the author is taking the opportunity to explore the limits of radicalism both of himself (possibly herself) and his or her audience. The fable toys with the idea of regicide without actually endorsing it clearly as the right course of action for British

---

15 T.B. and T.J. Howell (eds.), *A Complete Collection of State Trials* (1809–26), XXII, 446. Abbreviated to *ST* hereafter.

radicalism. A similar point has been well made by Mark Philp in a discussion of the King Chaunticlere fable from a rather different perspective than mine. He suggests that the difficulty of exactly working out the politics of the fable may be the result of its author 'playing with ideas and principles' and the 'intellectual and emotional reflexes' of an emerging audience. Philp has insisted on the developing nature of radical ideology in the 1790s: the principles of the participants changed and responded to the shifting circumstances of the decade. I would suggest that the nature of the seditious libel law ought to be considered as one of those circumstances.[16]

Eaton was arraigned on a charge of seditious libel for publishing the fable of King Chaunticlere. The charge was specifically laid out as:

> intending . . . to represent our said lord the king as sanguinary, tyranni-cal, oppressive, cruel, and despotic; and thereby to stir up and excite discontents and seditions amongst the subjects of our said lord the king, and to alienate and withdraw the fidelity, affection, and allegiance, of his said majesty's subjects. (*ST*, XXIII, 1014)

However, because of the nature of the law of seditious libel it was not enough for the prosecution simply to show that the fable was capable of causing disturbance. Fielding, the counsel for the prosecution, also had to demonstrate the libellous nature of the meaning specifically intended by Eaton. The interpretation favoured by the prosecution appears on the indictment in the form of parenthetical glosses. So the first reference to the 'game cock' is followed by '[meaning thereby to denote and represent our said lord the king]' (*ST*, XXIII, 1015). Each time in the fable the words 'despot' or 'tyrant' occur a similar gloss appears. The prosecution's interpretation of the fable was that it was an allegory of the imagined execution of George III. As the prosecution informed the jury during the trial, if they could 'affix any other, than that very meaning that is put upon the whole of this sentence by the innuendoes' (*ST*, XXIII, 1022) Eaton would have to be acquitted.

The prosecution lawyer was well aware that the defence would stress the incongruity of identifying the King with a game cock: 'good God! the advocate may say (because an advocate can always affect astonishment), why should you suppose the king is meant by this cock?' (*ST*, XXIII, 1029). He was well aware because the government recognised the use of 'flimsy concealment' (*ST*, XXIII, 1024) as

---

[16] Philp, 'The Fragmentary Ideology of Reform', pp. 70–2.

essential to the rhetoric of popular radicalism. And, indeed, Gurney, the defence lawyer, mounted exactly the arguments anticipated by the prosecution – rubbing salt into the wound by admitting that it was an age of seditious libel but feigning incredulity that, with so many libels about, the government had 'set themselves to work to make one' (ST, XXIII, 1032). The rest of Gurney's defence goes on to take each of the innuendoes in turn and show that they cannot be taken to refer specifically to George III. Indeed Gurney argued that the whole fable alluded to 'tyranny in general' or 'Louis the sixteenth in particular' (ST, XXIII, 1038) neither of which could be classed as seditious.

Gurney ridiculed the interpretation of the fable put forward by the prosecution. He claimed that if Eaton was convicted 'Aesop's Fables, is the most seditious book that ever was published':

> There is scarcely a fable that will not furnish an indictment. One of them occures to me at this moment; it is the fable of the Ape, who was made king. To punish him for his presumption in aspiring to that character, the fox led him into a trap; and when reproached by the ape for disloyalty, he went off with a sneer, saying, "You a king, and not understand a trap?" – Put this fable into an indictment, and call it a "scandalous, malicious, inflammatory, and seditious libel, of and concerning our severeign lord the king"; state in the innuendoes that the ape is intended to denote our said lord the king; and that not understanding trap, means ignorance of the regal functions; and garnish all this with "against the peace of our said lord the king, his crown and dignity"; and then you have patched up a most notable libel. With this receipt for drawing indictments, I could go through the book, and draw five hundred (ST, XXIII, 1038).

Gurney noted likewise that publishing biblical stories of wicked kings could lead to the situation whereby 'a man may be prosecuted for publishing the sacred scriptures themselves'. If Gurney's remarks are taken at face value, they might represent, as John Barrell would have it, the philosophical radical's firm belief in the propriety of the transparent language of Reason. Yet it is equally possible that there is a knowing humour in Gurney's comments since radicals, including Eaton himself, regularly published fables and extracts from the Bible for political ends.

The work of Annabel Patterson has recently emphasized how politicized the fable was as a form in the seventeenth and early eighteenth century, a form which was deemed appropriate to situations in which restrictions on the freedom of speech demanded self-protection. However Patterson has also suggested that John Gay's *Fables*, the most famous collection of the form from later in the eighteenth century, may 'represent a reclamation of the genre from occasional political satire or partisan debate for what appears to be a transparent and indeed crystalline moralism of the most general kind'.[17] It is possible that Gurney's attitude to the connection between fable and politics reflects the consequences of just such a reclamation. If his comments are taken at face value then he is suffering from a cultural amnesia about the earlier politicized tradition which is the main focus of Patterson's study. To accept this thesis would be to suggest that the political fable was a form which had disappeared from the public discourse of philosophical radicalism, but remained part of the more artisan culture of 'unrespectable' radicals like Eaton. The evidence is uncertain, but it is not impossible to find these kind of social rifts within the radicalism of the period even when one man is acting in the defence of another.[18]

Claims about Eaton's own attitude are easier to make with confidence since there is evidence that he was very much aware of the advantages of a form like the fable in the context of the legal procedures covering the statute of seditious libel. Three issues before 'King Chaunticlere' was published, the following lines appeared in *Politics for the People* under the title 'What Makes a Libel?: A Fable':

> In Æsop's new made World of Wit,
> Where Beasts could talk, and read, and write,
> And say and do as he thought fit;
> A certain fellow though himself abus'd,
> And represented by an Ass,
> And Aesop to the Judge accus'd
> That he defamed was.
> Friend, quoth the Judge, How do you know,
> Whether you are defam'd or no?
> How can you prove that he must mean
> You, rather than another Man?
> Sir quoth the Man, it needs must be,

---

17 Patterson, *Fables of Power: Aesopian Writing and Political History* (Durham, NC, 1991), p. 149.
18 On the potential differences between radical patrons and their less respectable associates, see Iain McCalman's comments, *Radical Underworld*, p. 84.

> All Circumstances so agree,
> And all the Neighbours say 'tis Me.
> That's somewhat, quoth the Judge, indeed;
> But let this matter pass,
> Since twas not Æsop, 'tis agreed,
> But Application made the Ass.

The poem advertises the fact that the law of seditious libel forces the prosecution to show a determinate malicious intent. The court cannot find a libel on the basis of a potential or even publicly accepted interpretation if that signification does not have the force of an exclusive and intended meaning. These lines indicate that Eaton published 'King Chaunticlere' in full awareness of the protection potentially afforded by the fabular form.[19]

Moreover the poem also anticipates Gurney's ironic observation at Eaton's trial that the prosecution had been forced to produce or invent the libel itself. Not only is it 'all the Neighbours' who see the plaintiff in the ass, the 'fellow' himself has to argue for the likeness. Gurney similarly enjoyed the irony in court of suggesting that it was the prosecution that was guilty of seditious libel since it chose to identify George III with King Chaunticlere. Perhaps this coincidence should be taken as evidence that Gurney himself must have fully understood the political advantages of fable which he pretended to mock in court.

Certainly other more respectable radicals besides Eaton were alive to the legal conditions under which their literature operated and, indeed, to the particular appropriateness of the fabular tradition to their situation. Thomas Spence's *Pig's Meat or Lessons for the Swinish Multitude* (1793–5) was a periodical very much like Eaton's *Politics for the People*. Among his lessons for the swinish multitude, Spence published two pages under the title 'Examples of Safe Printing'. The first example comprised the following lines from *The Faerie Queene* (Book V; Canto ix.i):

> To prevent misrepresentation in these prosecuting times, it
> seems necessary to publish every thing relating to Tyranny
> and Oppression, though only among brutes, in the most
> guarded manner.

---

[19] The lines were published by Eaton in *Politics for the People*, vol. 1, part 1, no. v, p. 53.

The following are meant as Specimens:–
That tyger, or that other salvage wight:–
Is so exceeding furious and fell,
As wrong
[Not meaning our most gracious sovereign Lord the King, or
the Government of this country]
when it hath arm'd himself with might;
Not fit 'mong men that do with reason mell,
But 'mong wild beasts and salvage woods to dwell
Where still the stronger.
[Not meaning the Great men of this country]
doth the weak devour
And they that in boldness doe excell,
And draded most, and feared by their powre.

Tampering with the literary authority represented by Spenser (including spelling the Elizabethan poet's name as 'Spencer' so as to make it more similar to his own) is typical of Spence's delight in appropriating the culture which Burke believed was beyond the swinish multitude. It is also possible that Spence was consciously alluding to Spenser's own place in the long tradition of political fable which has been excavated for the modern reader by Patterson. What is central for the purposes of this article, however, is Spence's knowing parody of the form taken by legal innuendoes.[20]

Indeed it seems possible that Spence was specifically thinking of Eaton's trial when he published this piece, because his quotation from Spenser is immediately followed by Spence's version of one of Aesop's fables. The glosses Spence provides again ostensibly deny a radical meaning in a kind of parody of Gurney's claim that Aesop could not be political:

THE LION AND THE OTHER BEASTS
From Æsop's Fables

THE Lion [not meaning our Sovereign Lord the King] and several other beasts, [not meaning the continental Kings and Powers] entered into an alliance offensive and defensive, and were to live very socially together in the forest [not meaning in Europe]. One day having made a sort of excursion, [not meaning in France] by way of hunting, they took a very fine, large, fat deer, [not meaning

[20] See *Pig's Meat*, third edition, 3 vols. (London, 1800), II, 14–15.

Dunkirk, Toulon, or any other place taken from the French] which
was divided into four parts; there happening to be then present, his
Majesty the Lion [not meaning as said before, our Sovereign Lord
the King] and only three others.

In this particular instance, the negative glosses of course indicate
precisely what *is* rather than what *is not* meant. The particular strategy
may have even been suggested to Spence by Justice Rose's summing
up at Eaton's trial:

> A man may use such language, as in the plain terms of it as first may
> appear to be no libel; but yet, perhaps, by looking into some other
> expression, or taking the intention of the party in the whole of the
> book, it will be impossible not to see, that though he uses language
> that is ironical, yet that you perfectly understand, he means exactly
> the reverse of what he says. (*ST*, XXIII, 1050)

Spence's strategy of inversion is scarcely sophisticated in this particular instance. That the fable mocks the war effort is obvious. The main
import of the piece, however, does not really seem to lie in the
particular meaning of this fable. It is primarily, as the title of the
section indicates, an 'example of safe printing'. The fable demonstrates a method to be followed. Spence is parodying and highlighting
the prosecution's need to attach specific innuendoes to libellous texts.
The fable is being promoted as a form which allows interpretative
indeterminacy to be exploited to the frustration of this requirement.
Both Eaton and Spence published fables which did not come with any
glosses: leaving their readers to decode what radical sentiments they
could, while resisting the attempts of the courts to fix them with a
seditious interpretation. 'The Lion and other Beasts' ends with a word
of advice to Spence's readers:

> Let us thus, O ye humbled Britons, be careful to shew what we do
> not mean, that the Attorney General may not, in his Indictments,
> do it for us.

Spence's *Pig's Meat* did not expect its readers to remain humbled. The
statement is ironically recommending ways to obstruct the Attorney
General. Saying 'what we do not mean' is part of a broader strategy of
not saying explicitly what we mean: resorting to irony, fable, and the
rhetorical resources of language.

Conclusion

Elsewhere I have written of popular radicals such as Eaton and Spence as bricoleurs who responded to the critical situation of the 1790s by creating an eclectic rhetoric of opposition from the cultural materials that lay at hand.[21] Unlike Barrell's philosophical radicals, their rhetoric tends to abjure the Enlightenment dream of a language transparent in relation to Truth. Eaton and Spence were subversive in the very techniques they exploited in that they continually worked through received structures like the fable form. I have suggested in this essay that one of the determinants of this strategy was the law of seditious libel, implemented in such a way that figurative and ironic rhetoric created interpretive difficulties for the prosecution, so increasing (though by no means guaranteed) the chances of an acquittal. I am not, of course, suggesting that this was the only determinant on popular rhetoric. The delight in taking received texts, plots, and forms and giving them (often tantalisingly) radical applications, as with Spence's treatment of Spenser and Aesop, seems to be part of a desire to subvert received textual authority. The complexities of the texts which responded to the possibility of a popular radical literature opened up in Paine's *Rights of Man* have scarcely been examined, despite the great deal of research done by historians on the events and ideologies of the 1790s. Even Olivia Smith's *The Politics of Language* tends to dismiss (with the exception of Spence's work) most of the popular radical writing of the decade. Any broad survey is certainly beyond the scope of this article. But recognizing the often sophisticated ways in which it responded to the conditions of censorship it had to face is at least a beginning.[22]

---

[21] See my *Dangerous Enthusiasm: William Blake and the Culture of Radicalism in the 1790s* (Oxford, 1992).
[22] See Olivia Smith, *The Politics of Language 1791–1819* (Oxford, 1984). Iain McCalman's *Radical Underworld* seems to have provided a fillip for literary scholars to do more work in this direction. See forthcoming work by Marcus Wood and David Worrall.

'What if to her all this was said?'
Dante Gabriel Rossetti and
the silencing of 'Jenny'

JOSEPH BRISTOW

I

IN THE CROSS-FIRE OF bawdy puns that animates *The Merry Wives of Windsor*, Parson Evans sets the young William Page before the boy's mother and Mistress Quickly. He wants William to display his knowledge of Latin pronouns. 'What', asks Sir Hugh, 'is your genitive case plural?' And he elicits this stuttering reply: 'Genitive case? . . . *horum, harum, horum*'. Shocked by this recitation, Quickly finds herself unable to control her tongue. 'Vengeance of Jenny's case!' she cries, 'Fie on her! never name her, child, if she be a whore', and she ignorantly declares how alarmed she is to hear that William has been taught to 'hick' (*hic*) and 'hack' (*haec*) – that is, to hiccup from excess drink – as well as learn to speak of prostitutes.[1] To her untrained ear, a pronoun instantly becomes a product of the tavern, and a grammatical form can do nothing but conjure up the image of a whore. It almost goes without saying that in misconstruing a schoolboy's Latin for English immorality Mistress Quickly debases both the classics and the vernacular, and her stupidity invites our merciless laughter. But it is her altogether more subversive function to disclose that the schoolroom is perhaps not so far from the brothel, and that an education in Latin shall not preserve boys like William from lewd desires. His struggle to articulate the genitive plural declines, so to speak, into a prostitute's pudenda. This is the quibbling 'case' that here enables an erudite young man's privileged speech to disclose his lust for a woman's body, even if what he says is worded in the wrong language.

This amusing scene provides one vivid instance of how scholarship and sexuality can interact in confounding ways. My immediate

---

1 William Shakespeare, *The Merry Wives of Windsor*, ed. T.W. Craik (Oxford, 1989), IV. i. 52–60. Craik suggests that 'hick' and 'hack' may also be laden with sexual innuendo: 180.

concern, however, is with a highly controversial Victorian poem that takes Mistress Quickly's words as its epigraph. First published in his 1870 volume of *Poems*, Dante Gabriel Rossetti's 'Jenny' depicts a learned young man's overnight encounter with a female prostitute. By framing 'Jenny' with a line from *The Merry Wives of Windsor*, Rossetti is drawing on Shakespeare's cultural authority to legitimize his poetic interest in a highly sensitive topic that drove at the heart of the Victorian social conscience. But Rossetti hardly continues in Shakespeare's vein of ribald wit. His long monologue is, to be sure, ponderously sombre. Elizabethan bawdy soon adopts the tone of high Victorian seriousness as the thoughtful young man laboriously displays his scholarship by alluding in turn to the classics, the Bible, and *Paradise Lost*.[2] The style of 'Jenny', too, moves at a noticeably halting pace. Lumbering trochees strain the alliterative first line ('Lazy laughing languid Jenny'), just as a gloomy half-rhyme jars the second ('Fond of a kiss and fond of a guinea'). It took Rossetti more than twenty years to redraft couplets of this kind, and in so doing he changed the direction of a major current in Victorian poetry. The poem certainly made a sufficient mark to warrant being quoted by Ezra Pound in 'Hugh Selwyn Mauberley'.[3]

'Jenny', without doubt, builds on the achievements made by the dramatic monologues that Alfred Tennyson and Robert Browning began to publish in the 1830s. Rossetti's poem first took shape in 1847–48 when he was in his late teens. In its earliest version, the speaker's direct address to the prostitute resembles the dramatic form shared by Tennyson's Ulysses and Browning's Duke of Ferrara. 'Jenny mine how dar'st thou be / In the nineteenth century?' (66–67),[4] asks

---

[2] Quotations from Dante Gabriel Rossetti's poetry are taken from *Poems and Translations 1850–1870* (London, 1919). Further references to line numbers appear in parentheses. The silent speaker of 'Jenny' compares the prostitute to the Paphian Venus (362); he alludes to the Gospel according to Matthew on three occasions (100, 316, and 323); and he refers to *Paradise Lost* IV: 800 (282).

[3] I am referring to the section 'Yeux Glauques', where the narrator invokes an age when Swinburne and Rossetti were 'still abused': Ezra Pound, *Selected Poems* (London, 1975), 101.

[4] Rossetti's 1847–48 version of 'Jenny' amounts to 130 lines and is printed in Paull F. Baum, 'The Bancroft Manuscripts of Dante Gabriel Rossetti', *Modern Philology*, 39 (1941), 47–68. Line references to this draft of the poem are given in the text. The manuscript of the 1869–70 revision is held by the Fitzwilliam Museum, Cambridge.

Rossetti's scholarly young man of Jenny who rests sleepily upon his knees. Her position within this poetic structure would seem to be like that of Ulysses's sailors or the envoy whom the Duke is enchanting as he discusses the portrait of his last Duchess. These implied auditors – precisely because they are implied – remain silent. But the relations between the speaker and the addressee in this type of poem are never entirely clear cut, and in any case these poems do not follow identical patterns. In 'Ulysses', for example, there appears to be a possible transition from interior thoughts to public speech. Exactly who is listening, and how they are responding, to the voices dramatized within such poems frequently remains within the realm of speculation.

Yet what is vital about Tennyson's and Browning's handling of the dramatic possibilities of the poetic 'I' is that it exerts altogether new pressures on the assumptions of authenticity previously invested in the voice expressed by the traditional lyric. Combining, in their own distinct ways, lyricism and dramatic speech, Tennyson and Browning brought a novel type of subjectivity into English poetry, one that allowed formerly unheard voices to express themselves. In Browning's hands, the religious casuist, the homicidal maniac, and the sexual adventurer – to name but three – are repeatedly subjected to an unsettling irony that actively encourages us to read between their lines. There are usually two incompatible sides to these often eccentric speakers, and their speech – which issues towards an often ill-defined implicit listener – serves to demonstrate a gap between rhetorical intention and auditory effect. The verbal gestures of Browning's personae often signal a desperate struggle with language which results in vexatious self-questionings. The more they speak, the more they find that they are subverting their aims by saying more than they perhaps intend. As Dorothy Mermin puts it, 'their obsessive concern with what they have or haven't said, will or won't say, generally retards the action and is often the centre of the plot.'[5]

Rossetti's poem, in both its first and last versions, shows a clear concern with the reflexive inquiries that feature so largely in these earlier dramatic monologues. But in 'Jenny' one aspect of the dramatic speaker's status preoccupied him more than anything else. As 'Jenny' underwent its major phase of revision in the late 1850s, the already equivocal status of the dramatic speaker's sense of being heard bore

<hr />

[5]   Dorothy Mermin, 'Speaker and Auditor in Browning's Dramatic Monologues', *University of Toronto Quarterly*, 45 (1976), 139.

heavily upon his text. Indeed, the 1848–49 draft signals some anxiety about the speaker's voicing of his thoughts: 'Nay, wherefore should such things be said?' (58), he asks, indicating that he is puzzled about exactly what is motivating his speech. But at no point does Jenny venture a reply, and the subsequent changes to the poem suggest that Rossetti was working in a context where the problem of the auditor was not simply one about the spectral place of an addressee conjured only by the force of rhetorical questions. Rossetti's relentless emendations to his poem, which persisted as his final proof sets went through the press, point to a much larger difficulty with dramatizing the poetic 'I'. He decided to make it entirely clear that the prostitute was not a suitable listener to his young man's thoughts. And so, over the years, he chose to make his protagonist mute – in so far as the final version of his poem emphasizes that we are reading the speaker's mind, instead of words freely expressed in public. In 'Jenny', Rossetti turned the dramatic monologue back to front by making his speaker as silent as Tennyson's and Browning's auditors.

Rossetti had good reason for placing his scholarly protagonist under this explicit ban of silence. Unlike earlier Victorian poets and novelists, Rossetti explores this polemical topic from the position of a male client who spends the night in the company of a prostitute, and who to some degree identifies with her plight. In placing his young man in such close proximity to Jenny, Rossetti came up against severe prohibitions surrounding what he wanted to say. Ruskin, for one, made his reservations clear. Writing in 1859, he declared that the batch of poems that Rossetti had shown to him were indisputably 'great'.[6] 'But', he adds, 'I should be sorry if you laid them before the public entirely in their present state'. 'Jenny' gave him the greatest trouble. Its 'too great boldness for common readers' discouraged Ruskin from passing the poem on to the *Cornhill Magazine* whose editor, William Makepeace Thackeray, would undoubtedly have rejected it. In 1870, writing to Frederic Shields, Rossetti remarked that 'Jenny' 'gave [James] Smetham a shock when I read it to him; but I was sincerely surprised on the whole at its doing so in his case, though I know many people will think it unbearable.'[7] Similarly, when responding to his mother's wish to know what was the 'good' of such a poem, Rossetti

[6] John Ruskin, 'To Dante Gabriel Rossetti', 1859 [?], in William Michael Rossetti, *Ruskin, Rossetti, Preraphaelitism: Papers 1854 to 1862* (London, 1899), 233–34.
[7] Rossetti, 'To Frederic James Shields', 11 April 1870, *Letters of Dante*

stated that there was 'not a particle of morbid imagination in it, no idealizing of vice.'[8] In the face of such disapproval, silence was in part Rossetti's novel technique to make his young man's thoughts heard. Since his eloquent speaker observes that he cannot articulate his private desires aloud, the poem appears to be involved in a double bind that typifies a prevalent attitude towards sexual representation within modernity. In this respect, the poem belongs to a discourse of sexuality stemming from the mid-nineteenth century where, as Michel Foucault observes, society 'speaks verbosely of its own silence', and 'takes great pains to relate in detail the things it does not say'.[9] 'Jenny' articulates what it is not supposed to express, and so, paradoxically, finds its voice.

This shift from public speech to private thought, therefore, may well be regarded as not simply an avant-garde aspect of Rossetti's poetic practice that would, for example, pave the way for women poets, such as Augusta Webster and Amy Levy, to dramatize the prostitute's own words in print.[10] Countless letters indicate that the long period of composition caused him great anguish – to the point that for many years he abandoned his poem altogether. In fact, before undertaking to silence his speaker in his 1859–60 draft, he desired to muffle the poetic voice so much that he sent it literally to the grave. Bound together with the drafts of all his early poems, 'Jenny' was laid in the coffin of his wife, Elizabeth Siddall, who died from an overdose of laudanum in February 1862. In consigning his poems to Siddall's grave, part of him was symbolically laid beside his dead wife. Yet this sacrifice was not total. Seven and a half years later, eager to retrieve his early works, he took great pains in arranging for her body to be exhumed. Exactly how we might interpret this astonishing act is certainly open to question. But one thing is for sure. He felt ambivalent

Gabriel Rossetti, eds Oswald Doughty and John Robert Wahl, 4 vols. (London, 1965), II, 837.
8 Oswald Doughty, A Victorian Romantic: Dante Gabriel Rossetti, second edition (London, 1960), 440.
9 Michel Foucault, The History of Sexuality, Volume One, An Introduction, trans. Robert Hurley (Harmondsworth, 1981), 8.
10 Augusta Webster, 'A Castaway' in Portraits, third edition (London, 35–63, and Amy Levy, 'Magdalen' in A Minor Poet and Other Poems (London, 1884), 70–71. These poems are discussed in the broader context of Victorian women's poetry on prostitution in Angela Leighton, ' "Because Men Made the Laws": The Fallen Woman and the Woman Poet', Victorian Poetry, 27 (1989), 109–27.

about whether these poems should occupy the private or the public sphere. Once the exhumation was over, Rossetti informed Ford Madox Brown: 'They are in a disappointing state. The things I have already, seem mostly perfect, and there is a great whole through all the leaves of *Jenny*, which was the thing I most wanted.'[11] This poem about the strong pull of sexual desire is, then, only too clearly linked to a specific kind of authorial possessiveness. And his strong wish to put these works into print was matched by his discomfort at the thought of their unfavourable reception.

Poems emerged from a period of intense writing activity spurred by his adulterous relationship with Jane Morris. This affair flourished in the years immediately after Siddall's death. It was in the mid-1860s, too, that his output in paintings was prolific, marking a high point in his career. Having previously shunned public scrutiny, he now demanded its attention, and it is reasonable to claim that he felt he was better placed than before to achieve renown as a poet. The differing markets for both poetry and painting certainly would appear to have intimidated him. Hardly anyone beyond his family and friends, together with a handful of enthusiastic patrons, came into contact with his productions. His longstanding reluctance until the late 1860s to exhibit his paintings in galleries suggests his unease in setting himself before the public eye, and he repeatedly resisted pressure from his patrons to meet fixed deadlines. Rather, many aspects of his life seem to have been founded in gaining the consent of others to meet his extraordinary needs. Biographers argue that it was the excitement generated by the first sonnets comprising 'The House of Life' published in the *Fortnightly Review* in 1868 that encouraged him to gather his earliest drafts together. In this bid for success, Rossetti ensured that his supporters reviewed *Poems* in practically all the most influential periodicals. The volume sold exceedingly well, passing into no less than three reprintings within the first year of publication.

Knowing full well that 'Jenny' would 'raise objections in some quarters', Rossetti assured Charles Eliot Norton that his poems had 'been written neither recklessly nor aggressively (moods which I think are sure to result in the ruin of Art), but from a true impulse to deal with subjects which seem to me capable of being brought rightly within Art's province.'[12] Determined to have respectability conferred on his handling of prostitution, Rossetti was assuredly working under

11 'To Ford Madox Brown', 14 October 1869, *Letters*, II, 752.
12 'To Charles Eliot Norton', 11 April 1870, *Letters*, II, 838.

the pressures of censorship, ones that intensified in 1857 when the Obscene Publications Act became law. Walter Kendrick notes how the passing of Lord Campbell's Bill affected George Eliot during the writing of *Adam Bede* in 1858. She withheld a plan of chapters from her publisher, John Blackwood, because any outline she might give of a narrative concerning illicit sexual relations and infanticide might be considered 'highly objectionable'.[13] The silence of Rossetti's speaker, then, may well point to the poet's fears about being ruined as an artist. Had this poem contained the merest suggestion of sexual intercourse, the chances were that he would have stood trial for intending to 'deprave and corrupt' his readers. (This is the widely interpretable formulation that Lord Justice Cockburn applied to obscenity legislation in 1868, and which remains on the statute books to this day.)

Yet fear of prosecution is certainly not the main reason that explains his scholarly young man's incapacity to speak out loud, causing him to refrain from even embracing Jenny. This muted voice is located in a cultural form that educated Victorians increasingly recognized as feminine. Poetry, by midcentury, had lost much of its Romantic authority, and countless reviews reveal the extent to which poetry was thought to be destabilizing the supposedly natural opposition between the sexes. The Pre-Raphaelites, even if comprising a very diverse group of men, in particular presented an image that was, by varying degrees, altogether too bohemian, flamboyant, and emotional for a society that took increasing notice of the kinds of athletic masculinity propounded by the Christian Socialists.

It is fair to say that Victorian poetry by middle-class men underwent, more than any other literary genre of its time, a process of feminization. Carol T. Christ has emphasized the centrality of the feminine subject in mid-nineteenth-century poetry by men, and Rossetti's poems and paintings certainly demonstrate the greatest concentration of interest by a Victorian male artist in alluring figures of femininity.[14] Equally concerned with the gendering of this genre, Mermin observes that for most Victorian periodical reviewers poetry

---

[13] Walter Kendrick, *The Secret Museum: Pornography in Modern Culture* (New York, 1987), 119–20. For the Eliot letter, see 'To John Blackwood', 1 April 1858, *The George Eliot Letters*, ed. Gordon S. Haight, 9 vols. (New Haven, CT, 1954–78), VIII: 201.

[14] Carol T. Christ, 'The Feminine Subject in Victorian Poetry', *ELH*, 54 (1987), 385–401.

was implicitly a kind of 'woman's work'.[15] Demanding easeful lyricism, readers of poetry assumed that the finest work was generally expressive, forever expanding a repertoire of sympathies associated with the angelic wife cherished by proponents of 'woman's mission.' In aiming to bring prostitution within the province of art, Rossetti did not wish to sound reckless or aggressive like the young men championed by the likes of Charles Kingsley. (In fact, throughout the late 1840s and 1850s, Kingsley had been keeping a very close eye on the issue of proper masculine vitality in poetry.[16]) Artistic men, thought Rossetti, should not stamp and shout to make their opinions known. They were altogether more refined than that. Yet, in being so tactful, restrained, and quietly spoken, they risked sounding effeminate. Browning found Rossetti's 'scented' poems, with their 'obsolete forms' and 'archaic accentuations', wholly disagreeable. 'I hate the effeminacy of his school', he complained in the year that Poems was published.[17]

Similar remarks were made by Robert Buchanan in 'The Fleshly School of Poetry', published under a pseudonym in The Contemporary Review in 1871. Buchanan's sensationalizing account of Pre-Raphaelite fleshliness might be readily dismissed as a piece of self-publicizing bombast. To all intents and purposes, it was simply that – the acidulated outpouring of a minor poet who wanted more attention than he was due from a prurient public, and who probably knew more than he should of Rossetti's sexual liaisons with Jane Morris. But, for all its insincere posturing, Buchanan none the less displays a deepening prejudice among Victorian reviewers that male poets were increasingly lacking in virility, and this is undoubtedly one of the main anxieties experienced by Rossetti's silent speaker. In any case, Buchanan had already contributed to the furore that exploded when Algernon Charles Swinburne published Poems and Ballads in 1866. In that year, he made almost identical charges to the ones he laid against Rossetti half a decade later: 'How old is this young gentleman', he asks, 'whose bosom, it appears, is a flaming fire, whose face is as the

[15] Mermin, 'The Damsel, the Knight, and the Victorian Woman Poet', Critical Inquiry, 15 (1986), 67.

[16] See, for example, [Charles Kingsley,] 'The Bothie of Toper-Na-Fuosich', Fraser's Magazine, 39 (1849), 103–10, and 'Alexander Smith and Alexander Pope', Fraser's Magazine, 48 (1853), 452–66.

[17] Robert Browning, 'To Isa Blagden', 18 June 1870, Dearest Isa: Robert Bronwnng's Letters to Isabella Blagden, ed. Edward C. McAleer (Austin, TX, 1951), 336.

fiery foam of flowers, and whose words are as the honeyed kisses of the
Shunamite.' He then draws a demeaning picture of Swinburne as the
beautiful but treacherous 'Absalom of modern bards, – long-
ringletted, flippant-lipped, down-cheeked, amorous-lidded'.[18]
'Namby-pamby' was the epithet Buchanan used in 1871 when complaining about the 'walking gentlemen of the fleshly school'.[19]

Buchanan, then, was not alone in denouncing Rossetti's indulgence
in emotion, as well as associating the poet's intense sensuality with a
lack of masculine strength. Comparing Rossetti's fleshly art with Si-
meon Solomon's homoerotic paintings, Buchanan remarked: 'There is
the same thinness and transparence of design, the same combination
of the simple and the grotesque, the same morbid deviation from
healthy forms of life, the same sense of weary, wasting, yet exquisite
sensuality; nothing virile, nothing tender, nothing completely sane'.[20]
Although Buchanan states that 'Jenny' is 'in some respects the finest
poem in the volume' – an opinion with which most reviewers would
agree – he is dissatisfied with it because of his 'constant suspicion
that we are listening to an emasculated Mr Browning'.[21]

In his forceful reply, 'The Stealthy School of Criticism', Rossetti
made his thoughts about 'Jenny' just as clear as he had to several of his
acquaintances before publishing Poems. His remonstrance provides by
far his firmest statement of intent, especially where both the status
and function of his silent speaker are concerned:

> Neither some thirteen years ago, when I wrote this poem, nor last
> year when I published it, did I fail to foresee impending charges of
> recklessness and aggressiveness, or to perceive that even some
> among those who could really read the poem and acquit me on
> these grounds, might still hold that the thought in it had better
> have dispensed with the situation which serves it for framework.
> Nor did I omit to consider how a treatment from without might

18 [Robert Buchanan,] unsigned review, Athenaeum, 4 August 1866, 137.
19 'Thomas Maitland', [pseudonym of Robert Buchanan,] 'The Fleshly
School of Poetry', Contemporary Review 18 (1871), 343. For a detailed discussion of the controversy that was caused by Buchanan's essay, see
Christopher D. Murray, 'D.G.Rossetti, A.C. Swinburne and R.W. Buchanan: The Fleshly School Revisited', Bulletin of the John Rylands Library, 65: 1
(1982), 206–234, and 65: 2 (1983), 176–207.
20 [Buchanan,] 'The Fleshly School of Poetry', 337.
21 [Buchanan,] 'The Fleshly School of Poetry', 343–44.

here be possible. But the motive powers of art reverse the requirement of science and demand first of all an *inner* standing-point.
The heart of such a mystery as this must be plucked from the very
world in which it beats or bleeds; and the beauty and pity, the
self-questionings which it brings with it, can come with full force
only from the mouth of one alive to its whole appeal, – that is, of a
young and thoughtful man of the world.[22]

Carefully modified, his introspective monologue aimed to lend real-
ism to one of the most pressing mysteries of the day. But Rossetti did
not enjoy the last word on his art. Buchanan revised and extended his
essay, publishing it as a pamphlet in the spring of 1872. William E.
Fredeman infers that the widespread press reaction contributed to the
breakdown Rossetti suffered in June that year.[23] Already under the
influence of the chloral hydrate that he first used to cure insomnia,
Rossetti remained in a deranged state of mind for the whole summer.
The 'fleshly school' controversy indisputably left its stain on Rossetti's
later career, since the poem that Buchanan most despised, 'Nuptial
Sleep', was not reprinted in the volume of *Ballads and Sonnets* that
presented the poet's collected works to an increasingly appreciative
audience. William Michael Rossetti draws attention to the crucial
role played by Buchanan in driving the poet to the brink of suicide.[24]
The pain that 'Jenny' gave him from the time of Siddall's death to the
period of mental illness that occurred a decade later obviously reveals
his extreme sensitivity about his stature as a writer.

One particular feature of 'Jenny' would seem to bear out this point.
In this monologue, Rossetti draws up an implicit parallel between the
protagonist's words and the prostitute herself. Since the silent speaker
interprets the young woman as if she were a book, the poem takes on a
rather uncanny dimension. Just as he subjects Jenny to critical scrutiny, we too place his unspoken words under examination. The poem
is, then, situated before our gaze in the same manner that Jenny is to
the silent speaker. This structure of redoubled readings surely

22 Rossetti, 'The Stealthy School of Criticism', *Athenaeum* 2303, 16 December 1871, 793.
23 William E. Fredeman, 'Prelude to the Last Decade: Dante Gabriel
Rossetti in the Summer of 1872', *Bulletin of the John Rylands Library*, 53
(1970–71), 272n.
24 William Michael Rossetti, *Dante Gabriel Rossetti as Designer and Writer*
(London, 1889), 160, and *Dante Gabriel Rossetti: His Family Letters with a
Memoir*, 2 vols. (London, 1895), I, 305.

indicates that the poem in some ways figures as a prostitute, and she a poem. Both, after all, share the same name – Jenny. Both are shrouded in silence. It does not take much to see that not only the scholarly young man but also Rossetti's poem as a whole wish to protect themselves from the kinds of humiliation that the streetwalker suffers at the hands of the public. In the literary marketplace, 'Jenny' is in danger of suffering abuse, especially from the law and hostile reviewers like Buchanan. Hence Rossetti's attention to the '*inner* standing-point' from which the thoughtful young man speaks.

Rossetti's sense of his own artistic prostitution in the commercial market is substantiated in a revealing passing remark that Rossetti makes in a letter to Ford Madox Brown: 'I have often said that to be an artist is just the same thing as to be a whore, as far as dependence on the whims and fancies of individuals is concerned.'[25] And similar worries can be found in several of Rossetti's items of prose. Jerome J. McGann draws attention to the discernible tension between maintaining artistic integrity in the face of professional success in the fragment entitled 'St Agnes of Intercession' dating, like 'Jenny', from the late 1840s. There the young artist anticipates the response of visitors to the exhibition of his work; he feels he is 'submitting to them his naked soul, himself, blind and unseen.'[26] Encountering one's critics often struck Rossetti as tainting the purity of what he strove for in his art. In this respect, the poems he had been collecting since the earliest days of the Pre-Raphaelite Brotherhood had a special importance for him. As he wrote to William Allingham: 'I suppose one's leaning still to them depends mainly on their having no trade associations, and being still a sort of thing of one's own.'[27] Such comments lead McGann to conclude that the 'gift of his book of poems to Elizabeth [Siddall]'s corpse was a gesture that his artistic soul was alive, and that he still had the integrity to preserve its life.' Yet, perhaps like Jenny, his desire for an appreciative kiss, if not a public guinea, drove him back into the arms of an audience before whom he felt he was inevitably a whore.

Yet one must be cautious in drawing up this comparison. The recurring identifications between the poem, the silent speaker and Jenny herself are far from straightforward, and the divergent critical

[25] 'To Ford Madox Brown', 28 May 1873, *Letters*, III, 1175.
[26] Jerome J. McGann, 'Dante Gabriel Rossetti and the Betrayal of Truth', *Victorian Poetry*, 26 (1988), 340.
[27] 'To William Allingham', September or October 1860, *Letters*, I, 377.

readings of this monologue point to the perplexity that frequently arises when scholarship is brought to bear on sexuality. These analyses are, indeed, so much at odds that one begins to see how 'Jenny' provides a useful example of a literary work that discloses that the critical project is in itself always engaged in allowing some things to speak while consigning others to silence. I should like to argue that whenever critical dissension of this kind occurs it is likely that the text we are reading is trying to come into possession of the very problem with which we find ourselves grappling. Our analysis, in other words, begins to mime the impasse we may encounter in reaching judgements about what is being said and what is left unspoken, from the title, through the epigraph, and then in each and every line.

The second part of this essay looks at how the related issues of reading prostitution and reading poetry preoccupy a poem consciously developed beneath the pressure of censorship. The personal and social constraints under which 'Jenny' was produced point to the persistent difficulties that emerge when reaching critical judgements about sexual representation. Since it is so attentive to what can and cannot be said about sexual desire, 'Jenny' is historically located at the beginning of a modern understanding of sexuality – especially in terms of obscenity and pornography – from which we have not yet extricated ourselves. Sexuality is still mystified by the forms of censorship that seek to suppress it. 'Jenny' can give us some idea why.

II

Let me, then, outline the narrative of Rossetti's poem in its 1870 version. Having left his room 'so full of books' (23), the silent speaker appears to be a something of a latterday version of the grown-up William Page. Musing upon the beautiful young woman, Rossetti's protagonist recalls how 'hour by hour the books' in his library 'grew dim' (45), and why he decided to leave his 'cherished work' to go dancing (27). Now that he has returned to Jenny's rooms, she slumbers in his lap, and the rest of the poem is given over to an extended meditation on what her life as a prostitute represents for him, and what he imagines it means to her. At times, his response takes the form of sympathetic identification. He regrets her subjection to the 'daily jeer and jar' of schoolchildren (80). On other occasions, he expresses misogynistic disgust at her defilement within an economy where her genitals have become her 'purse', and her predatory body forms a 'Grim web. . .clogged with shrivelled flies' (341–42). Subjected to his fantasy, she transmogrifies from a woman who could have served as a model for Raphael or Da Vinci (238) to an irredeemable whore with a 'desecrated mind, /Where all contagious currents meet' (164–65). She is both purity and danger, beauty and the beast, madonna and magdalen in one, and he experiences considerable difficulty in distinguishing one aspect from another. Having let these thoughts pass, the silent speaker scatters gold in her hair. This is a gesture that, he knows, resembles the shower of gold that Zeus bestowed on the Danae, and which substitutes for the seed that he has not – in Victorian slang – been able to 'spend'. The early draft suggests that his reluctance to consummate this relationship stems from his impotence, and this once again has some bearing on the problem of poetic authority. In the occasionally broken grammar of this incomplete version, it appears that the speaker is suggesting that his 'words' and their 'dusty sense' are 'Rocked in their wretched impotence' (64–65).[28] But this feeling of impotence would be, in the course of revision, withdrawn from the text, as he gazes on the sleeping Jenny and as we eavesdrop on his private thoughts about her.

Not unsurprisingly, 'Jenny' has received critical attention from several feminist critics investigating male representations of Victorian womanhood, and this poem undoubtedly provides a remarkably rich source of material for comprehending how and why the dichotomy between the virgin and the whore repeats so persistently in mid-nineteenth-century writing. Placing her emphasis on different radical feminist accounts of pornography, Robin Sheets shows how this literal writing about prostitutes 'displays men's social, economic, and sexual power, denies women's subjectivity, and orders ways of seeing'.[29] Using details from Swinburne's often lurid correspondence with Rossetti,

---

[28] The Bancroft manuscript of 'Jenny' is least clear where the word 'impotence' appears. The fractured grammar permits 'impotence' to be attributed to Jenny as well, since the verb 'Rocked' can be viewed as dependent on those preceding verbs that relate to the 'pages' of Jenny's brain. I take up the issue of grammatical indeterminacy in the 1870 version in much greater detail below.
[29] Robin Sheets, 'Pornography and Art: The Case of "Jenny" ', *Critical Inquiry*, 14 (1988), 317. Recent feminist commentaries include Helena Michie, *The Flesh Made Word: Female Figures and Women's Bodies* (New York, 1987), 59–61, and Elizabeth K. Helsinger, 'Consumer Power and the Utopia of Desire: Christina Rossetti's "Goblin Market" ', *ELH*, 58 (1991), 921.

Sheets bases part of her essay on a parallel between 'Jenny' and the sexual violence represented in the Marquis de Sade's *Justine* (1791). (De Sade's novel had been a topic of conversation between the two men while the poem was undergoing its final phase of rewriting.[30])

Sheets claims that the poem is organized around the relationship between an empowered male subject and a violated female object. The speaker exercises his interpretative authority over the bodily text of the prostitute. Discerning the silent speaker's 'increasing animosity' towards Jenny,[31] Sheets lays greatest emphasis on the way the young woman's 'silence is essential to provoke his soliloquy', and suggests that in the course of his meditation the silent speaker abrogates his 'responsibilities' towards the prostitute: 'At no point does the narrator define himself as artist, poet, or author of a text'.[32] And to substantiate her claims Sheets draws on Steven Marcus's view that Victorian pornography 'typically undertakes to represent itself not as a story or fantasy but as something that "really" happened'.[33] Marcus's comments join with the claims of radical feminist critics who believe that pornography witnesses the collapse of representation itself – in so far as it forms an exact substitute for reality. (Susanne Kappeler, for example, states that 'the fiction [i.e. pornography] continues its existence in reality'.[34] No distinction should be made between the two, since that would enable liberals to allow acts of sexual violence against women directly caused by pornography to continue unabated.) On this view, pornography achieves an unmediated relationship between spectator and spectacle allowing all moral considerations to be abandoned. In sum, Sheets argues that it is the silent speaker's utter failure to recognize his agency in the economic and sexual system of prostitution that renders his monologue pornographic.

By contrast, Daniel A. Harris's equally exhaustive investigation of 'Jenny' stresses from the outset that this work is 'Rossetti's indictment of prostitution and male attitudes toward sexual exploitation', leading

---

[30] Algernon Charles Swinburne, 'To Dante Gabriel Rossetti', 19 February 1870, *The Swinburne Letters*, ed. Cecil Y. Lang, 5 vols. (New Haven, CT, 1959), II, 96–98.

[31] Sheets, 'Pornography and Art: The Case of "Jenny" ', 319.

[32] Sheets, 'Pornography and Art: The Case of "Jenny" ', 331.

[33] Steven Marcus, *The Other Victorians: A Study of Sexuality and Pornography in Mid-Nineteenth-Century England* (London, 1966), 46.

[34] Susanne Kappeler, *The Pornography of Representation* (Cambridge, 1986), 10.

ultimately to the exposure of Jenny's 'dehumanization'.[35] This approach follows a line of essays that claim, like D.M.R. Bentley, that the 'thrust of . . . the entire poem . . . is that evil is an immutable feature of post-lapsarian time that will vanish only at the apocalyptic death of the world.'[36] But Harris examines Rossetti's presumed dissatisfaction with the lust of the world by focussing on the silent nature of the speaker. He accounts for the speaker's silence by imagining the effects that spoken words might have on the young woman. Quoting the two lines that accentuate the young man's anxiety at being heard – 'Suppose I were to think aloud, – / What if to her all this were said?' (156–57) – Harris then engages in an elaborate series of speculations about the replies the young woman *might* make if she listened to this interpetation of her life. His imaginary projection of her possible responses accounts for the protagonist's inability to venture these thoughts out loud:

> If the protagonist actually spoke to Jenny awake, he would have to accept her responsive speech; her possible replies (dramatic monologue invites the reader to imagine the auditor's response) suggest the pressures the protagonist experiences so uneasily. If, indeed, 'to her all this were said', her answer – whether grateful or hostile – would create precisely the linguistic, and thus human, bond the protagonist fears. First, Jenny might thank the protagonist for his understanding, welcome his sexual restraint, and tell him the pathetic history he barely intuits. This conventional response, palatable to a conservative ideology, would maintain the status quo of prostitution, male domination, and the use of sympathy in place of social reform. But the protagonist's response to this own thought of speaking 'aloud' – vindictively comparing Jenny's mind to a sewer or vagina contaminated by sexual disease (165–69) – suggests that he anticipates an explosive or hostile reply.[37]

Just as the speaker entertains thoughts of Jenny's life of prostitution, so too does Harris attempt to enter into her consciousness. It is as if Harris's critique uncannily replicates the very problem he is attempting

[35] Daniel A. Harris, 'D.G. Rossetti's "Jenny": Sex, Money, and the Interior Monologue', *Victorian Poetry*, 22 (1984), 197, 205.
[36] D.M.R. Bentley, ' "Ah, Poor Jenny's Case": Rossetti and the Fallen Woman/ Flower', *University of Toronto Quarterly*, 50 (1980), 177.
[37] Harris, 'D.G. Rossetti's "Jenny": Sex, Money, and the Interior Monologue', 202.

to analyze. He concludes by stating that 'this scenario . . . helps explain why Jenny's silence cancels the protagonist's fear of censorship'.[38] I believe that Rossetti's poem prompts this kind of reaction because the silent speaker labours under an obligation not to cause offence, and consequently produces a discourse which occupies a realm where sexuality becomes an object that thwarts critical understanding.

More vividly than any other figure of the Victorian period, the prostitute condenses this confusion about sexual representation. Countless nineteenth-century commentators attempted to account for what led this woman into her world of work. Some claimed it was her overproductive reproductive organs, others stated that it stemmed from the always already fallen nature that she inherited from Eve. The lack of agreement between these commentators is astounding. Subject to increasing investigation by doctors (William Acton and W.R. Greg), historians (W.H. Lecky), and journalists (Bracebridge Hemyng), the prostitute became the most uninterpretable – and, by virtue of that, repeatedly interpreted – emblem of sexual desire.[39] Her sexuality was endlessly produced through a medico-moral textuality that subjected her mind and body to all sorts of contradictory theories. Rossetti's poem bears the traces of these competing explanations, and that is why the silent speaker veers so wildly from loving to loathing what Jenny seems to represent. But this monologue is unlike most other accounts in so far as it reflects on how the prostitute might respond to this range of attitudes. Its self-consciousness makes it unique.

In proceeding from quite different premises about Rossetti's poem, Sheets and Harris significantly depart in their apprehension of its strikingly self-conscious poetic form. In his review of 1871, H. Buxton Forman observes that the poem is unique because of the speaker's apparent silence: 'It is perhaps a question rather for artists than for critics, how far the monologue may be allowed to include *thoughts* that are unspoken; and, as far as we know, *Jenny* is the only poem of any importance in that form wherein such a question is raised.'[40] Mindful

---

[38] Harris, 'D.G. Rossetti's "Jenny": Sex, Money, and the Interior Monologue', 203.
[39] There is a large corpus of critical material on Victorian prostitution. The standard work is Judith Walkowitz, *Prostitution and Victorian Society: Women, Class, and the State* (Cambridge, 1980).
[40] [H. Buxton Forman,] 'Dante Gabriel Rosetti, Poet', *Tinsley's Magazine*, 8 (1871), 159.

of this point, Harris views Rossetti's production of an 'interior monologue' of this type – one that 'breaks the ground from Eliot's "The Love Song of J. Alfred Prufrock" ' and subsequent Modernist works – as an ideal model for marking 'the speaker's ethical crisis'.[41] Harris believes that the silence that Rossetti's protagonist imposes on himself intensifies the conflicted feelings experienced by the erudite young man for the prostitute. Even though he pays attention to the numerous instances when the silent speaker expresses his sexual disgust at Jenny, Harris claims that the structure of silence makes Rossetti's 'audacity in speaking out all the more impressive'.[42] Lodging her own reading in part against Harris's essay, Sheets comments in a footnote that for the purposes of her work 'it does not matter if the young man is speaking or thinking; he is organizing language for his own ends'.[43] Sheets, then, readily dismisses one of the founding principles of Harris's argument. In fact, their readings reach opposite conclusions because they attend to differing aspects of the poem's regime of silence. But they are similar in assuming that the position from which their chosen silence should be understood is entirely clear. For Sheets, the speaker censors Jenny; for Harris, the speaker censors himself.

The deadlock between these two very different analyses is to a large extent broken by a third intervention. In her essay on questions of agency in 'Jenny', Amanda S. Anderson concentrates on Rossetti's deliberate negation of the dramatic monologue, and how within this framework we witness an extraordinary oscillation between the protagonist and his female 'other'. Anderson concludes that 'moves to *fix* the other are unbalanced by reversals that locate agency in Jenny', and that the poem 'displays the way in which the presence or fact of another consciousness not only produces moves to stabilize or foreclose but also continually thwarts such moves.'[44] And it is the silent speaker's desire to read Jenny that activates extremely intricate moments of intersubjectivity. Rather like an intractable work of literature, Jenny tests the limits of the erudite young man's interpretative

[41] Harris, 'D.G. Rossetti's "Jenny": Sex, Money, and the Interior Monologue', 197.
[42] Harris, 'D.G. Rossetti's "Jenny": Sex, Money, and the Interior Monologue', 315.
[43] Sheets, 'Pornography and Art: The Case of "Jenny" ', 318n.
[44] Amanda S. Anderson, 'D.G. Rossetti's "Jenny": Agency, Intersubjectivity, and the Prostitute', *Genders*, 4 (1989), 119.

powers. Asleep in his lap, she resembles a volume taken down from his library shelves: 'You know not what a book you seem, / Half-read by lightning in a dream!' (51–52). These lines certainly signal the difficulty he has in maintaining a direct system of address towards her. Set before him, her 'warm sweets open to the waist' (49), Jenny hovers between her literal status as a woman and her figurative representation as a book.

Everywhere, the poem entwines the compulsions of sexual desire with the activity of reading, particularly the puns, ambiguities, and uncertainties that derive from the silent speaker's hermeneutic interests. Not content to compare Jenny to a book, his mind settles for some time on a different kind of text, one in which she might feature. 'Jenny' contains a single reference to pornography – the 'book/ In which pure women may not look' (253–54). The prostitute is said to be like a 'rose shut' between its pages. What turns out to be an extended simile points in two directions. In one respect, the book crushes the rose. It destroys her purity. But in another sense, the 'rose shut' in there is captured forever. Like a pressed flower, her original beauty is preserved for the pornographer's delectation. Yet in this moment when the scholarly young man comes closest to aligning his monologue with a pornographic work, he disavows his immediate desire for such 'base pages'. Having declared that 'pure women may not look' at obscene publications, he goes back on his word by musing on the response that would be aroused if 'pure women' fixed their gaze upon their fallen sister. And so he engages in a reading of a respectable woman examining a book he has already claimed is not designed for her:

> its base pages claim control
> To crush the flower within the soul;
> Where through each dead rose-leaf that clings,
> Pale as transparent psyche-wings,
> To the vile text, are traced such things
> As might make lady's cheek indeed
> More than a living rose to read;
> So nought save foolish foulness may
> Watch with hard eyes the sure decay;
> And so the life-blood of this rose,
> Puddled with shameful knowledge, flows
> Through leaves no chaste hand may unclose:
> Yet still it keeps such faded show
> Of when 'twas gathered long ago,

That the crushed petals' lovely grain,
The sweetness of the sanguine stain,
Seen of a woman's eyes, must make
Her pitiful heart, so prone to ache,
Love roses better for its sake: –
Only that this can never be: –
Even so unto her sex is she. (255–75)

This single complex sentence ceaselessly shifts identifications between the pure rose, the crushed rose, and the male reader – the
object that is read, the subject who reads, and the voyeur who witnesses them both. As this system of relations surely indicates, the
layers of interpretation thicken as the poem guides itself closer and
closer to thinking about the naked female body.

Although one can easily grasp the silent speaker's fascination with
the embarrassment experienced by the respectable lady when she
gazes on the likes of Jenny, the passage suggests a likeness between
these ostensibly different women, making them appear equally corrupt. Not only crushed within, but also clinging to the 'vile text', the
spectacle of the 'dead rose-leaf' causes the pure woman to blush,
bringing a rose-coloured hue to her cheeks. Anderson helpfully points
out that the rose functions as a mutable emblem, one whose status
quickly alters through grammatical slippages. Noting the problem of
attributing agency to the verb 'traced', she remarks that the 'things'
that offend the respectable woman reader could be put there by either
the 'vile text' or the 'lady' herself.[45] Throughout this excerpt, it is
unclear who or what brings about corruption. On the one hand,
reading pornography contaminates the chaste mind of the pure
woman. But, on the other, the image of the rose articulates so much
about *both* the stain that it leaves on these 'base pages' *and* the colour
that it brings to a 'lady's cheek' that one might follow Anderson's
suggestion that the rose itself is an already corrupted medium, and
that there may not be any original purity at all. In other words, this
metaphor implies that pornography does not make women fall from
grace, since they are – as women, as roses – already fallen.

The closing lines of this long extract bring the note of indecision
more explicitly to the fore. Are we to think that the sight of the
'crushed petals' lovely grain' is likely to move the respectable woman

---

[45] Anderson, 'D.G. Rossetti's "Jenny": Agency, Intersubjectivity, and the
Prostitute', 117.

to tears, arousing her pity? By way of an answer, the erudite young man offers two qualifications. But these statements compound his present difficulties. 'Only that this can never be', he interjects. If the force of this negation is entirely clear, its frame of reference is certainly not. The demonstrative 'this' could mean *either* that she would never be reading such 'base pages' in the first place *or* that reading the 'vile text' would not arouse her sympathy. The final axiom – 'Even so unto her sex is she' – consequently impels us towards alternative conclusions. Even if this clause means that she is consistent in her womanliness, the qualities that define 'her sex' have been remarkably unsettled by the preceding lines, since the rose that defines femininity may appear *either* corrupted *or* corrupting. Little wonder, then, that the speaker, in turning his attention once more to Jenny, considers the prostitute 'A riddle that one shrinks / To challenge from the scornful sphinx' (281–82). Here the prostitute is *both* an agent of her mystery (like the sphinx, she offers the riddle) *and* the product of one (she is imaged as a sphinx). Either way, her femininity proves to be a puzzle. The more the silent speaker reflects on what he is reading, the more he confounds himself.

Anderson concludes that 'the erotic state issues out of a crisis in intelligibility', and that 'reading is linked with desire'.[46] I would wish to extend this point by noting that textuality and sexuality are closely interwoven here because a modern type of sexual fantasy emerges most forcefully within a conspiracy of silence that serves to mystify the object of desire, and in so doing generates even more desire. By taking one of the most reviled figures for his subject-matter, Rossetti had to extend a poetic form that would allow him to speak of being unable to speak – to the point that one might claim that this self-conscious interrogation of silence becomes one of the main preoccupations of 'Jenny'. This negativity ensures that the discourse on the unspeakable prostitute becomes exceptionally long-winded, if not syntactically indecisive. But this aspect of Rossetti's poem does, I think, require further theorization, otherwise all that will remain is the duplication of the intellectual problem in which this monologue is enmeshed.

The marked difficulty of ascribing agency to many sections of 'Jenny' can be illuminated by referring to the psychoanalytic category

[46] Anderson, 'D.G. Rossetti's "Jenny": Agency, Intersubjectivity, and the Prostitute', 118.

of fantasy. In the strict Freudian sense of the term, fantasy does not
involve the subject taking up a fixed role in relation to the object.
Rather, fantasy enables the adoption of a range of positions and
identifications within what may be termed a staging of images. In
their influential discussion of this concept, Jean Laplanche and Jean-
Bertrand Pontalis comment:

> Fantasy . . . is not the object of desire, but its setting. In fantasy the
> subject does not pursue the object or its sign: he appears caught up
> himself in the sequence of images. He forms no representation of
> the desired object, but is himself represented as participating in the
> scene although . . . he cannot be assigned any fixed place in it.[47]

One example from 'Jenny' should clarify how the sequence of images
keeps these fantasmatic mechanisms in play. Early in the monologue,
the silent speaker recalls 'the wild tunes that spun' Jenny round (6).
Anderson brilliantly prompts the thought that this line implies a pun
on the 'spinning Jenny'.[48] Like a piece of industrial machinery, the
prostitute is involved in a repetitive world of work. Indeed, much of
the monologue refers to turning and spinning. But these allusions are
not purely concerned with Jenny's mechanical servitude to her
clients. They also reveal the restless nature of this monologue where
the subject takes up one role and instantly relinquishes it for another.
The spinning motion that he attributes to the prostitute stands as a
metaphor for the perpetual whirling motion of his fantasy.

Sexual representation surely demands that we attend to the
mobility of positions understood within fantasy. Failure to do so will
only ensure that sexuality continues to be produced by a highly jud-
gemental and moralistic discourse which claims that the relations
between subject and object are crystal clear, and that no ambiguity
disrupts them. For all the meticulousness of their readings, Sheets's
and Harris's analyses add up to two commonplace responses to the
question of speaking about sex. On the one hand, Sheets draws on
radical feminist accounts that assume that the male subject imposes
his will on the female object, thus showing how Rossetti's poem
perpetuates sexual oppression. On the other, Harris adopts a liberal

[47] Jean Laplanche and Jean-Bertrand Pontalis, 'Fantasy and the Origins of
Sexuality' (1964), in Victor Burgin, James Donald, and Cora Kaplan, eds.,
Formations of Fantasy (London, 1986), 26.
[48] Anderson, 'D.G. Rossetti's "Jenny": Agency, Intersubjectivity, and the
Prostitute', 106.

line that accepts that poets are made virtuous by their art, and that
poetic innovation in itself provides sufficient grounds upon which to
judge the poet's progressive responses to prostitution (Rossetti's 'incipient feminism').[49] But the poem, as Anderson's essay helps to explain, cannot easily occupy either side of this divide. It points instead
to a crisis in comprehending what it is that prevents sexuality from
being freely expressed, and what enables fantasy to occur under the
cover of censorship.

Rossetti's poem does not, I believe, require critical approval or
disapproval, since such divisive understandings keep it within much
the same legal discourse that argues whether or not a publication is
obscene. To be lured into estimations of the poem as either emancipatory or oppressive is to enact the same fantasmatic processes that
inform its structure. These are, indeed, dangerous premises on which
to evaluate its political intentions and effects. Modern criticism must
resist participating in this logic of praise and blame, or else it will
remain driven along two parallel paths. In one respect, it will lead to
more campaigns to ban sexual representations that are claimed to
cause harm, assuming that male fantasy is damaging to women. While
in another sense, it will encourage a libertarian stance, assuming that
the endless exhibition of such representations will normalize them.
Rather, 'Jenny' needs to be read for what it is: an acutely unresolved
monologue that articulates the conditions that have brought about
this double bind. It speaks, almost interminably, of the silence surrounding its desires. 'What if to her all this were said?' Instead of
answering this question, literary critics would profit from considering
the circumstances which have led to its formulation, both specifically
within the shifts and transformations of Victorian poetry and generally within the culture at large. If this point goes unnoticed, then
Rossetti's readers are left more or less abandoned to the uncompre-
hending exclamations of Mistress Quickly, who unhesitatingly
misreads Jenny's 'case' and jumps to the most surprising conclusions.

[49] Harris, 'D.G. Rossetti's "Jenny": Sex, Money, and the Interior Monologue', 204.

'The pools, the depths, the dark places': Women, Censorship and the Body 1894–1931

KATE FLINT

IN THE SPEECH which she gave to the *National Society for Women's Service* early in 1931, Virginia Woolf told her audience a version of how she came to be a writer. She began, she said, by writing reviews. Behind her shoulder, right from the beginning, was that idealised, oppressive figure of the Angel in the House, cajoling her to be sympathetic, tender, and flattering; to carry private virtues of willing self-sacrifice into a public arena. She was, after all, reviewing a book written by a man, for a paper owned by men, edited by men. But she refused to give way. Every time she felt the shadow of her wings or the radiance of her halo upon the page she flung the inkpot at her. She killed her, in the end. So, 'now that she had rid herself of falsehood, that young woman had only to be herself. Ah, but what is "herself"? I mean, what is a woman? I assure you, I do not know; I do not believe that you know'.[1] In the first instance, Woolf relates the question of identity to public performance. She will not be able to 'know' woman 'until she has expressed herself in all the arts and professions open to human skill'. But she soon indicates that to know woman will necessarily involve representing her in all her aspects. This was impossible for the young novelist she once was, and she thought it impossible for women at the time she was speaking:

> I want you to figure to yourselves a girl sitting with a pen in her hand, which for minutes, and indeed for hours, she never dips in the inkpot. The image that comes to my mind when I think of this girl is the image of a fisherman lying sunk in dreams on the verge of a deep lake with a rod held out over the water. She was letting her imagination sweep unchecked round every rock and cranny of the world that lies submerged in the depths of our conscious being. Now came the experience, the experience that I believe to be far commoner with women writers than with men. The line raced

---

[1] Virginia Woolf, 'Professions for Women' (delivered 1931; revised version published in *The Death of the Moth* 1942), *Virginia Woolf: Women & Writing*, ed. Michèle Barrett (London, 1979), p. 60.

through the girl's fingers. Her imagination had rushed away. It had
sought the pools, the depths, the dark places where the largest fish
slumber. And then there was a smash. There was an explosion.
There was foam and confusion. The imagination had dashed itself
against something hard. The girl was roused from her dream. She
was indeed in a state of the most acute and difficult distress. To
speak without figure she had thought of something, something
about the body, about the passions which it was unfitting for her as
a woman to say. Men, her reason told her, would be shocked. The
consciousness of what men will say of woman who speaks the truth
about her passions had roused her from her artist's state of uncon-
sciousness. She could write no more. The trance was over. Her
imagination could work no longer.

For Woolf, the problem of 'telling the truth about my own experiences as a body, I do not think I solved. I doubt that any woman has
solved it yet'.[2]

Writing *The Pargiters* in the autumn of the following year – the
work which was to split into *The Years* and *Three Guineas* – Woolf
demonstrated the difficulty of writing about the male as well as about
the female body. Rose, a girl of ten, goes out in the dusk to the local
shop to buy some toy swans. She passes a man on the way there; on
her way back she sees him leaning against the pillar box. 'There was
nobody else anywhere in sight. As she ran past him, he gibbered some
nonsense at her, sucking his lips in & out; & began to undo his
clothes . . .'.[3] In the essay which follows the chapter containing this
incident, Woolf comments both on the instinctual feeling of guilt
which subsequently came over Rose – a sense of guilt and of a need for
concealment which, she asserts, the girl had in common with novelists of the nineteenth century, and which had prevented them writing
about the true nature of such experiences – and about the prohibitions under which she herself wrote. For her, the problem is not one of
personal prudery, but:

there is, as the three dots used after the sentence, "He unbuttoned
his clothes . . ." testify, a convention, supported by law, which
forbids, whether rightly or wrongly, any plain description of the
sight that Rose, in common with many other little girls, saw under

2 Ibid., pp. 61–62.
3 Virginia Woolf, *The Pargiters*, ed. Mitchell A. Leaska (New York, 1977),
p. 43.

the lamp post by the pillar box in the dusk of that March evening. All the novelist can do, therefore, in order to illustrate this aspect of sexual life, is to state some of the facts; but not all; and then to imagine the impression on the nerves, on the brain; on the whole being, of a shock which the child instinctively conceals, as Rose did; and is also too ignorant, too childish, too frightened, to describe or explain even to herself, as again Rose was.[4]

In these passages, Woolf draws on two arenas in which censorship operates: a public, legislative one, and a more intimate site, that of self-censorship. Self-censorship can be both deliberate, doing the work of the state for it in order to ensure the publishability of a work, or, in the sense that Woolf is interested in here, it can be performed in the unconscious. Freud adopted the term 'Zensur' from the discourse of public legislature to describe the selective barrier between the unconscious and the preconscious-conscious systems, thus placing the concept of censorship at the point of all repression. What may be said to join the social sphere with an individual's psychological functioning is ideology: or rather, as Woolf shows here through the way in which she passes without distinction from one to the other, the function of ideology, in this respect, is to collapse the boundaries between the two. Simultaneously, the differences between the literal and metaphorical uses of the word 'censorship' are dissolved.

Bodies are not abstractions, but are sites accreted with cultural expectations. The history of each body asks to be read in relation not just to the perceptions of the mind which simultaneously is contained within it and figures it, but in relation to other bodies, and thus to the further sets of expectations which are consequently generated. Woman does not write solely from the private knowledge gained through inhabiting a gendered body, but from a socialized position, experiencing, as well as challenging or reinforcing, the daily cultural construction of 'womanhood'. When Woolf wrote about the difficulty of telling 'the truth' about her own experiences as a body, what did she have in mind? At one level, she is writing of an upbringing shared in outline with countless other girls of her generation. The artist Laura Knight (born 1877), for example, recalls how her training as an artist was affected by prevalent views of propriety. As a student in Nottingham during the early 1890s: 'if the men worked from the

4 Ibid., p. 51.

living figure I had to go into the Antique Room',[5] no nude models being provided for any women students at the art school. Moreover, although not having the same advantages in professional training as her male counterparts, she felt bound to take on board the same type of academically serious subjects as they, not painting what lay immediately to hand: 'had I only had the sense to know, there were subjects in plenty right where I was: my sister's and my own life. If sense of propriety had not interfered, I would have painted Sis taking her bath every morning in a little flat, round bath-tin placed in front of the studio coal-fire'.[6] The depiction of women's self-contained habitation of intimate domestic space – getting dressed, putting on make-up, looking at themselves in the mirror – became a frequent theme of women's painting between the wars, but for Knight, and for her close contemporary Dod Procter, this depiction went against the grain of what had been thought fitting for them as a woman to paint.

More specific autobiography may have driven Woolf's preoccupations. Rose's concealment and shame may be a reflection of her own reaction to the abuse she suffered at the hands of her half-brother, Gerald Duckworth.[7] Or perhaps, when alluding to 'the passions which it was unfitting for her as a woman', she had in mind heterosexual or maternal desires, or menstruation, or perhaps her recent relations with Vita Sackville-West, or perhaps her earlier feelings for Violet Dickinson. The absence of precise reference may be an act of conscious or unconscious self-censorship: we cannot tell, there being no self-proclamatory blank space on the page inviting our speculation. Yet refusing to be specific should not be read here as a limitation: rather, she enabled listeners and readers to supply whichever of their own experiences are most resistant to verbalization, as well as hinting more generally at women's ingrained inhibitions.

'All we ever know of censorship are its failures', Christian Metz has remarked. But, as he goes on, 'the reverse is equally true, and perhaps more important: the failures of censorship establish the knowledge we have of it'.[8] Yet knowledge of its existence may not simultaneously

5   Laura Knight, The Magic of a Line (London, 1965), p. 77.
6   Ibid., p. 98.
7   See further Louise De Salvo, Virginia Woolf: The Impact of Childhood Sexual Abuse on her Life and Work (London, 1989), esp. pp. 185–90.
8   Christian Metz, Psychoanalysis and Cinema. The Imaginary Signifier, translated by Celia Britton, Annwyl Williams, Ben Brewster and Alfred Guzzetti (London, 1982), p. 255.

reveal or explain its mechanisms. We can see this if we examine the first draft of *A Room of One's Own* – initially entitled *Women and Fiction* – which Woolf composed in March 1929. Particularly telling is the section in which she imagines a novel, in which 'Chloe' is first a character, then a writer:

> <'I read'> "Chloe liked Olivia; they shared a ___" <the words came at> the bottom of the page; the pages had stuck; while fumbling to open them there flashed into my mind the inevitable policeman; the summons; the order to attend the court; the dreary waiting; the Magistrate coming in with a little bow; the glass of water; the counsel for the prosecution; for the defense; the verdict; this book is obscene; & flames rising, perhaps on Tower Hill, as they consumed <that> masses of paper. Here the pages came apart. Heaven be praised! It was only a laboratory.'[9]

What *specifically* has flashed into Woolf's mind is the trial of Radclyffe Hall's *The Well of Loneliness* for obscenity: a trial at which she had offered to give evidence in the novel's favour. She made this offer not because she believed in the book's literary merit (rather, she wrote to Lady Ottoline Morrell that 'The dulness of the book is such that any indecency may lurk there – one simply can't keep one's eyes on the page –'[10]) but because she believed in the importance of freedom of speech, crucial when even the normally liberal *New Statesman* could claim that Hall made a mistake in writing the book at all, 'for people who desire toleration for pathological abnormalities certainly should not write about them'.[11] Although in the final version of *A Room of One's Own* this reference to the trial shrinks to the dimensions of checking, before turning the page and reading that 'Chloe liked Olivia' that 'there are no men present? Do you promise me that behind that red curtain over there the figure of Sir Charles Biron [the presiding magistrate in *The Well of Loneliness* trial] is not concealed?',[12] the manuscript of *Women and Fiction* continues, a page later:

[9] Virginia Woolf, *Women and Fiction. The Manuscript Versions of 'A Room of One's Own'*, ed. S.P. Rosenbaum (Oxford, 1992), p. 114.
[10] Virginia Woolf to Lady Ottoline Morrell, early November 1928, *A Change of Perspective. The Letters of Virginia Woolf*, vol. 3, 1923–1928, Nigel Nicolson and Joanne Trautmann, eds. (London, 1977), p. 556.
[11] Unsigned piece in the *New Statesman*, 24 November 1928, quoted in Vera Brittain, *Radclyffe Hall. A Case of Obscenity?* (London, 1968), p. 115.
[12] Virginia Woolf, *A Room of One's Own* (London, 1929; Harmondsworth, 1945), p. 81. For a reading of *A Room of One's Own* based on its relation to

Now if Chloe likes Olivia <& can write,> something of great importance has happened, because this liking . . . will serves as a torch to light up that vast dark cave, where nobody has yet been, I thought. Chloe will say Olivia offers an extraordinary'

and here the manuscript breaks off in mid-sentence. Woolf starts a new page: 'She can tell us what women are like when they are alone'.[13] Yet she had just been complaining that what has been conspicuously lacking from literature is the representation of women's relations between themselves: how interesting it would have been if Shakespeare had made the relationship between Cleopatra and Octavia more complicated, for example, rather than conventionally falling back on jealousy as being the only emotion between them that could possibly count. And in raising *this* possibility, she made another telling slip of the pen or of syntactical logic, suggesting not just emotional attachment, but the importance of sexual sameness, in writing 'Chloe *like* [my italics] Olivia, but Cleopatra did not like Octavia.'[14] How may we go about describing these slippages, this suggestion of close companionship – or more – that is abandoned in favour of something far more decorous, if also difficult, in the 1920s to write about: the figure of a woman on her own, off-guard, in no way suspicious of observation? Did she realise that what she was about to write was potentially too explicit, too transgressive? But we are considering a text still in manuscript form: she was under no obligation to transfer the contents of notebook to typescript to printed page. In private, Woolf could certainly write suggestively about what two women may get up to when together, even if she had a tendency to use language which was not just metaphorical, but zoomorphic. 'To think of sporting with oysters', she wrote to Vita Sackville-West after spending a night at Long Barn: '– lethargic glaucous lipped oysters, lewd lascivious oysters, stationary cold oysters, – to think of it, I say . . . You only be a careful dolphin in your gambolling, or you'll find Virginia's soft crevices lined with hooks'.[15] Or was Woolf, in this draft

the trial of *The Well of Loneliness*, see Jane Marcus, 'Sapphistry: Narration as Lesbian Seduction in *A Room of One's Own*', in her *Virginia Woolf and the Languages of Patriarchy* (Bloomington and Indianapolis, 1987), pp. 163–187.

[13] *Women and Fiction*, pp. 116–117.

[14] Ibid., pp. 114–115.

[15] Virginia Woolf to Vita Sackville-West, 4 July 1927, *Letters of Virginia Woolf*, III, p. 395.

of a piece on women and writing, potentially sporting with her reader, as she had done a few paragraphs earlier, refusing to put into words the possibilities which she had just called up in her reader's mind? This has been suggested by Ellen Bayuk Rosenman in relation to the earlier passage: 'the secret space that the reader and the characters share before the turn of the page, the narrator's "fumbling" and her attempts to open the sticking pages, and the final coming apart suggest sexuality, labia, and an erotic experience that includes the narrator as well as the characters.'[16] Ludic censorship was certainly practised by her in personal (and, in the sense of shared understanding, Sapphic) correspondence: thus she wrote to Ethel Smyth about the great pleasure she has always found in reading: 'the state of reading consists in the complete elimination of the *ego*; and its the ego that erects itself like another part of the body I dont dare to name'.[17] Or did something well up in her own unconscious, and forbid her to find precise, as opposed to metaphorical language with which to describe bodily intimacy between two women?

The problem of finding, and publishing, adequate language to describe such intimacy was not Woolf's alone, and it is the lack of such language, or the inability to allow it voice in print, which has generated a good deal of recent debate about what constitutes lesbian identity in the first place, and, concomitantly, what might constitute a lesbian text. On the one hand is positioned Adrienne Rich, proposing a lesbian continuum of 'woman-identified experience', which allows in a large number of novels and poems positing the importance of intense friendships between women;[18] on the other, Catharine Stimpson is clear that for her, lesbian identity necessitates 'a commitment of skin, blood, breast, and bone'.[19] But to insist on this is not very helpful when it comes to considering writing of the past, particularly when it is impossible to determine whether conscious or unconscious self-censorship

---

[16] Ellen Bayuk Rosenman, 'Sexual Identity and *A Room of One's Own*: "Secret Economies" in Virginia Woolf's Feminist Discourse', *Signs: A Journal of Women in Culture and Society* 14 (1989), p. 637.

[17] Virginia Woolf to Ethel Smyth, 29 July 1934, *The Sickle Side of the Moon. The Letters of Virginia Woolf*, vol. 5 (London, 1979), p. 319.

[18] Adrienne Rich, 'Compulsory Heterosexuality and Lesbian Existence' in Ann Snitow, Christine Stansell, and Sharon Thompson, eds., *Powers of Desire* (New York, 1983), p. 192.

[19] Catharine R. Stimpson, 'Zero Degree Deviancy: The Lesbian Novel in English', in ed. Elizabeth Abel, *Writing and Sexual Difference* (Chicago, 1982), p. 244.

has been at stake. In *Surpassing the Love of Men. Romantic Friendship and Love between Women from the Renaissance to the Present* (1981), Lillian Faderman has shown how problematic it can be assessing the implications of intense friendships between women if we look back only with late twentieth century categories: can behaviour or writing which might seem overtly lesbian to us be so termed if those engaged in it would not have recognized or accepted such terms?

Written in the aftermath of Havelock Ellis and Krafft-Ebing's theorization, many of the portrayals of lesbians in fiction by Woolf's contemporaries are, as have frequently been noted, condemnatory and stereotypical.[20] The unnaturalness of Banford and Marsh's cohabitation in D.H. Lawrence's *The Fox* (1922) is underscored by the infertility of all the livestock on their farm; Clare, in 'Clemence Dane's' *Regiment of Women* (1915), the tall and mannish Mary, in Dorothy Sayers' *Unnatural Death* (1927), and the 'warped and stunted' Victoria Vanderleyden of Naomi Royde-Smith's *The Tortoiseshell Cat* (1925)[21] all are referred to in terms which indicate not just their predatory, but their vampiric tendencies. Mannish appearance in relation to 'unnatural practices' is continually mentioned in relation to the protagonists in Compton Mackenzie's *Extraordinary Women* (1928), a sneering caricature and roman à clef of the lesbian circle on Capri during World War One. Even Rosamond Lehmann's *Dusty Answer* (1927), which is in many ways extremely sympathetic towards Judith's intense feelings towards Jennifer, sets up a dichotomy between the naivete of the younger girl and the practices involved in the relationship Jennifer has with her older, crop-haired, masculine-jawed friend Geraldine. 'There are things in life you've no idea about. I can't explain', Jennifer tells Judith as she leaves Cambridge. For her part, Judith 'shrank from knowing'.[22] The reader is placed in her position, with only the Coleridgean hint – if she occupies, vicariously or otherwise, Judith's position of a student of literature – of the unspeakably sinister vision offered by the very name 'Geraldine'.[23]

[20] See, for example, Esther Newton, 'The Mythic Mannish Lesbian: Radclyffe Hall and the New Woman', *Signs*, 9 (1984), pp. 557–75; Sonja Ruehl, 'Inverts and Experts: Radclyffe Hall and the Lesbian Identity', *Feminism, Culture and Politics*, Rosalind Brunt and Caroline Rowan, eds. (London, 1982), pp. 15–36.
[21] Naomi Royde-Smith, *The Tortoiseshell Cat* (London, 1925), p. 310.
[22] Rosamond Lehmann, *Dusty Answer* (London, 1927; Harmondsworth 1984), pp. 179–180.
[23] In Coleridge's 'Christabel' (1797–1800), both the narrator and the young

But if one goes back a couple of decades, to the so-called 'New Woman' fiction of the 1890s, before medical theory ossified such stereotypes, the literary picture is more complex. Diana Fuss, in *Essentially Speaking* has argued that ' "lesbian" ' is not an unchanging, ahistorical, natural category, but 'a historical construction of comparatively recent date . . . there is no eternal lesbian essence outside the frame of cultural change and historical determination.'[24] But this does not make it any easier to define the relationships between women in, say, Emma Frances Brooke's *Transition* (1895), or Ethel M. Arnold's *Platonics* (1894), or Edith Johnstone's *A Sunless Heart* (1894). Had these books explicit physical scenes in them, they could confidently be claimed, of course, as counter-cultural texts. But either the physical contact is written about in terms which displaces the nature of the relations of the women concerned, or it is avoided. Thus in Brooke's novel, the close friendship between the headmistress and schoolteacher, Honoria and Lucilla, is seen at its most intense when Honoria, seeing Lucilla in distress, unlaces her boots, gives her a lecture about the true nature of emancipation – which consists, for her, in finding work that suits one and doing it well – and then cradles the other woman to her:

> I don't know how it is, Lucilla, but the sight of you stirs within me the prevision that I am a born mother – a caterer for a tableful of hungry naughty children, with my mind on jam and consolation. I am glad you are small. It makes it more dignified and fitting that I should kiss you, *thus*, squeeze you in my arms *this way* – as though you were a child.[25]

Ethel Arnold's widowed heroine, Susan, develops a rather different philosophy: one of asceticism, making herself believe that the root of all sin and misery lies in the imprisonment of the Soul within the walls of the Ego. But she cannot sustain this abstraction when her best friend, Kit, marries, and dies of a broken heart. Ostensibly, the reason

girl are dumb at the sight of Geraldine's unrobing: 'A sight to dream of, not to tell!/O shield her! shield sweet Christabel!' (Part I, 253–4).
[24] Diana Fuss, *Essentially Speaking* (London, 1989), p. 45.
[25] Emma Frances Brooke, *Transition* (London, 1895), p. 287. Although the plot of this novel has a heterosexual framework, it is very much subordinated to the narration of two independent women living in London, and their involvement not just with education, but with socialist and anarchist politics.

for this is that she, futilely, loved Kit's husband herself, but the letter she wrote her woman friend during the last moments of her life gives the lie to this: '. . . I am only conscious for my love for you. The past is all lit with it – I can't realize the time when it was not; it holds a torch up to the future – for its cessation is unthinkable'.[26] A different sort of love triangle is set up in Johnstone's novel, between the schoolteacher Lotus Grace, her Creole pupil, and the teacher and artist Gasparine. Although the nature of the relationship is more specific – the narrator breaks off to remind the reader that whilst it has so far been the province of the novel to deal with 'the passion of love' between man and woman, and the complications arising from it: 'this is only one side of life. There are others. In many lives such love plays but a minor part, or enters not at all. Will no one voice them, or find beauty in them? . . . I have tried to show, in all purity of intent, what women may be, and often are, to each other.'[27] 'In all purity of intent' is a difficult phrase: do we understand that Johnstone is making it clear that there's nothing wrong in a lesbian relationship, or that a close relationship between women may not involve genital contact, or simply that she wants to make it plain that she's not writing with sensationalist, salacious motives. How do we later interpret Mona's suggestion, when Lo tries to break off with her ('. . . the end is coming. Face it bravely. The end of fantastic dreams, and insecure existence. You will go into the world of ordinary sensations . . .') that they ' "go to the old inn, and sleep there together for to-night, our arms round one another in the way that was always my best rest" '?[28]

Yet the uncertainties raised by these texts lead to a further question: is censorship – whether imposed from within or without – necessarily a bad thing? Annette Kuhn, writing about cinema censorship between 1909–1925, suggests that it may not always be so. To consider censorship only in the light of prohibition, excision or 'cutting-out', she writes, is to fall into the belief that a censored text must distort 'reality' and must therefore, in some way, be partial in its representation. In turn, this assumes a subordination of representation to reality, yet 'to assume that censorship only prohibits or represses is to forget that censorship may equally well be *productive* in its effects.'[29] We should not, in other words, be trying to disinter some kind of

[26] Ethel Arnold, *Platonics* (London, 1894), p. 127.
[27] Edith Johnstone, *A Sunless Heart* (London, 1894), p. 148.
[28] Ibid., pp. 208–9.
[29] Annette Kuhn, *Cinema, Censorship and Sexuality* (London, 1988), p. 4.

'truth', some *a priori* actions or desires from the hints offered by these 1890s novels, so much as be paying attention to their suggestiveness.

In relation to the issues I've been discussing, it may here be helpful to look at some recent remarks made by Bonnie Zimmerman. Not only does she suggest that lesbianism may have a particular relationship to the operations of language in the work of representation: 'The lesbian, or any of her earlier avatars, may always have been constituted in metaphorical terms. Perhaps that is one of the particular contributions of lesbians: to disrupt what we accept as reality and suggest new connections between signs';[30] she connects this metaphorical power not with that which resides, essentially, within the text, but with the freedom which it may grant the reader. Whilst she acknowledges that it is important 'to research how women in the past may have understood themselves in relation to and against heterosexuality'[31] – something which involves, if only strategically, aligning oneself with essentialist assumptions about the continuation through time of a generalized lesbian subject, and which may be an empowering exercise – she also investigates the notion that 'lesbian textual practices create (or lesbian readers perceive) a *narrative* space in which writer and reader, or writer and assumed audience, or female characters, come together in a relationship defined as lesbian.'[32] Zimmerman grants this space the status of an imaginary topographical location: it is a space of free play, where boundaries between self and other, subject and object, lover and beloved may be seen to break down; where lesbian identity may be created as well as located. Yet this metaphor of space may be doubled up: 'space' not just being employed in the sense of bounded environment, but in the sense of an (invisible) textual gap. It is into this gap that a reader may insert herself: her desires, her imaginings, her figuration of a relationship between women that enables her to construct her own version of what may constitute lesbian identity, or identity as a woman: an identity the more fluid for not being named.

Censorship, we should not forget for a moment, can often be a practice of oppression, or a sign of repression. But the refusal, or the

30 Bonnie Zimmerman, 'Lesbians Like This and That', *New Lesbian Criticism. Literary and Cultural Readings*, ed. Sally Munt (Hemel Hempstead, 1992), p. 10.
31 Ibid., p. 9.
32 Ibid., p. 10.

inability, to 'tell the truth about [one's] own experiences as a body' may in fact be an enabling, rather than an inhibiting process. For neither the responses of bodies, nor the pulse and flow of the emotions, are stable and constant, as Woolf notes and demonstrates in both her private writings and her published fiction. Nor are they necessarily legible. Take, finally, the passage in *To the Lighthouse* where Lily recollects sitting close to Mrs Ramsay:

> Sitting on the floor with her arms round Mrs Ramsay's knees, close as she could get, smiling to think that Mrs Ramsay would never know the reason of that pressure, she imagined how in the chambers of the mind and heart of the woman who was, physically, touching her, were stood, like the treasures in the tombs of kings, tablets bearing sacred inscriptions, which if one could spell them out would teach one everything, but they would never be offered openly, never made public. What art was there, known to love or cunning, by which one pressed through into those secret chambers? What device for becoming, like waters poured into one jar, inextricably the same, one with the object one adored? Could the body achieve it, or the mind, subtly mingling in the intricate passages of the brain? or the heart? Could loving, as people called it, make her and Mrs Ramsay one? for it was not knowledge but unity that she desired, not inscriptions on tablets, nothing that could be written in any language known to men, but intimacy itself, which is knowledge, she had thought, leaning her head on Mrs Ramsay's knee.[33]

If Mrs Ramsay never knows the reason for that pressure, nor, for sure, do we. Does Lily see Mrs Ramsay as some version of Kristeva's 'phallic mother'?[34] Does she desire her physically, or seek to share in her power at a more metaphysical level? This passage is one which renders Woolf's later problematic, about the difficulty of 'knowing' women, in some respects redundant. Feeling, unity, recognisable only in that it lies beyond language, is here seen as superior to knowledge. To 'know', in these terms, is to name: to name is to put into language, and hence, potentially, to classify, to offer a hostage to legislation. It is, moreover, to create or fix a version of 'woman'. In this context, censorship, whether unconscious or deliberate, may be seen to have the potential

---

[33] Virginia Woolf, *To the Lighthouse* (London, 1927), pp. 82–83.
[34] See Julia Kristeva, 'Stabat Mater', *The Kristeva Reader*, ed. Toril Moi (Oxford, 1986), pp. 161–186.

for gain as well as for loss. In refusing to give words to sexual practices, to sexual feelings, to gendered identity, censorship can allow the reader to merge her own desires, experiences, and imagination with those which are suggested but unvoiced within the text. To do this means, valuably, destabilizing the boundaries suggested by Woolf's initial question 'what is a woman?'.

'Disgusted, Shepherd's Bush':
Brimstone and Treacle *at the* BBC

MARTIN WIGGINS

ANY DISCUSSION OF CENSORSHIP at the BBC will necessarily contain an element of speculation. All successful censorship makes its object invisible, but at the BBC the censorship itself is also invisible. The decision not to broadcast an item is entirely an internal matter, closed to public scrutiny and accountable to no outside body: there is no right of appeal, and there can be no informed public debate, since the BBC has no statutory obligation to explain its actions. This is one reason why the suppression in 1976 of Dennis Potter's television play *Brimstone and Treacle* did not become the *cause célèbre* that Potter evidently hoped. Other post-war censorship cases, such as the prosecutions of *Lady Chatterley's Lover* in 1960, *Oz* 28 in 1971, and *Gay News* in 1977, became notorious because the proceedings were conducted in open court, and people were therefore able to develop sophisticated opinions and write letters to *The Times* about them. In the case of Potter's play, however, there was only the impersonal and uninformative press announcement that, 'in the opinion of the BBC television service, *Brimstone and Treacle* ought not to be shown since it is likely to outrage viewers to a degree that its importance as a play does not support'.[1]

The case has also lacked the feeling of deprivation which successful censorship tends to incite, for Potter went to great lengths to circumvent the BBC ban and bring his play before a public audience. The script was published in the May 1976 issue of *The New Review*, and a stage adaptation was produced at the Crucible Theatre, Sheffield in the autumn of the following year; it was also performed in London early in 1979.[2] Potter then collaborated with Kenith Trodd, who had been the BBC's in-house producer of the play, to make a film version, which was released in 1982. Finally even the BBC relented, and

---

[1] BBC Spokesman quoted in *The Stage and Television Today*, 25 March 1976, p. 13.
[2] *The New Review*, vol. 3, no. 26 (May, 1976), pp. 31–51; quotations are from this edition, except where stated. The stage version was also published, in the Methuen New Theatrescripts series (London, 1978).

broadcast the original television production for the first time as part of a Potter retrospective in August 1987. In different forms, then, the play has been more widely available than many BBC drama productions which were not banned.

Brimstone and Treacle is a black parody of a popular genre best represented by the film *It's a Wonderful Life* (1946). It begins with suburban despair, and it ends with a miracle: in a climate of incipient marital break-up, Mr and Mrs Bates care for their daughter Pattie, reduced to a gibbering vegetable after a hit-and-run accident; and in the course of the action a charming and mysterious stranger, Martin, enters their lives, cures Pattie, and then disappears into the night. Familiar, perhaps, but with a twist: this time the household has not entertained an angel unawares. Where *It's a Wonderful Life* and its kind spooned out treacly sentimentality, Potter's play offers a touch of brimstone: the devil has all the best miracles.

The two unscripted epigraphs which punctuate the first scene are the best guide to this aspect of the play. First: 'There resides infinitely more good in the demonic man than in the trivial – Kierkegaard.' Then, with no variation of the voice-over speaker's tone: 'A spoonful of sugar helps the medicine go down – Andrews.'[3] Angel in the house is a syrupy role which Martin plays to win the Bates's confidence and with it an invitation to stay and help with Pattie. Once installed, he rapes her, and the shock restores her to mental normality; like medicine, it is nasty, but curative. The demonic man has done good in spite of himself.

Broadly speaking, it is understandable that the BBC should believe that offence might be caused if the play were transmitted. Rape, religion, and mental illness are all sensitive topics, but Potter does not treat them sensitively: they are the incidentals of the plot rather than the objects of reverent analysis; it is not a play 'about' those subjects. It does not follow from this, however, that the ban was justified. It is notable that Potter's efforts to get his play seen brought it, with more or less the same manifest content, into an arena where it was subject to the Obscene Publications Acts 1959 and 1964, the Theatres Act 1968, the judgement of the local licensing authorities for cinemas, and, informally, that of the British Board of Film Censors.[4] It was

[3] i.e. Julie Andrews, in the film *Mary Poppins* (1964).
[4] The BBFC had no power in law, though cinema licences usually required the exhibitor to abide by its recommended certificates; however, the licensing authorities always reserved the right to vary the certificate or ban a film

neither banned nor prosecuted, and this safe passage past the instruments of public censorship inevitably calls into question the BBC's private, institutional act of censorship in 1976.

Brimstone and Treacle was made at a time of reaction and retrenchment at the BBC: Kenith Trodd later characterized the 1970s as 'the censorship decade' for television, after the liberties of the 1960s.[5] Underlying the very different policies followed by the BBC in each of these decades was the Obscene Publications Act 1959, which expressly excludes BBC broadcasts from its scope.[6] Under Hugh Greene, the liberal intellectual Director-General appointed in 1960, this was interpreted as a licence to dare, and the result was the emergence of organized opposition in the form of the Clean-Up TV Campaign (later the 'National Viewers' and Listeners' Association'), a right-wing and extremist Christian pressure-group led by Mary Whitehouse. One of the central objectives of this group was a change in the law to make the BBC accountable to a Broadcasting Council.[7]

Greene's confrontational approach, then, entailed the risk of a political backlash that might cost the BBC its autonomy. The Corporation's interests were better served by seeking an accommodation with the protesters, and Greene's successor, Charles Curran (appointed in 1969) accordingly made a point of paying greater attention to Whitehouse, without necessarily acceding to her demands outright. The crucial *volte-face* was the issue in 1973 of new guidelines on taste and standards in BBC programmes.[8] The document recognized that, in the past, the BBC had made and broadcast outstanding programmes (*The Wednesday Play*, *Culloden*, and *Till Death Us Do Part* were named) which had 'come about through apparent defiance of accepted practice', and it did not repudiate their artistic success; but it was clear that, in future, the forestalling of public criticism was to have a higher priority. In other words, the BBC entered the mid-1970s determined

---

altogether. Many authorities had exercised this power two years before the film of *Brimstone and Treacle* was released, to prevent the showing of *Monty Python's Life of Brian*.

[5]   Quoted in Francis Wheen, *Television* (London, 1985), p. 118.

[6]   Broadcast performances in general are also excluded from the scope of the Theatres Act 1968. See also Michael Tracey and David Morrison, *Whitehouse* (London and Basingstoke, 1979), p. 144, for the opinion of the Director of Public Prosecutions on the feasibility of prosecuting the BBC on a charge of conspiracy to corrupt public morals or outrage public decency.

[7]   Ibid., ch. 8.

[8]   The full text was published in *The Times*, 8 February, 1973, p. 4.

to impose a narrower standard of acceptability, in the hope that it would be understood to be putting its own house in order without the need for legal or constitutional coercion.

Brimstone and Treacle was the first play that Dennis Potter submitted to the BBC after the issue of these guidelines.[9] The script was delivered in December, 1974, and was approved for production by the Head of Plays, James Cellan-Jones. The finished version was seen and approved by Bryan Cowgill, the Controller of BBC–1, and it was scheduled for transmission as part of the *Play for Today* strand on 6 April 1976. At the last moment, less than three weeks before the play was due to go out, and after the *Radio Times* for that week had gone to press, it was announced that *Brimstone and Treacle* would not, after all, be broadcast.[10] Alasdair Milne, BBC Television's Director of Programmes, had seen the play, and, repelled, decided to withdraw it from the schedules. He later wrote to Potter to explain his decision: 'I found the play brilliantly written and made, but nauseating. I believe that it is right in certain instances to outrage the viewers in order to get over a point of serious importance, but I am afraid that in this case real outrage would be widely felt and that no such point would get across.'[11]

This was, to say the least, an extraordinary way for the BBC to conduct its affairs, even allowing for its increased proneness to impose censorship at this time. Potter himself said as much in a grumpy article published soon afterwards in the *New Statesman*: for the Director of Programmes to ban a play which had been discussed and scrutinized for fifteen months at every level from tea boy to channel controller, and finally pronounced acceptable for transmission, looked alarmingly like a personal whim – and, when that play had cost around £70,000 to make, quite a costly whim at that.[12] The price tag signifies more, however: it may have been managerially inept to leave the decision so late, but even an inept executive does not knowingly waste so much money without a compelling reason. Milne was

9 The commission and. production of two other plays, *Joe's Ark* and *Schmoedipus* (both transmitted in 1974) overlapped with the guidelines.
10 This was the first time the BBC had dropped a *Play for Today*, and the decision makes a neat metonymy for the development of its policy at this time: the series, under its former title, *The Wednesday Play*, had been the Corporation's drama flagship during the Hugh Greene era.
11 Quoted by Dennis Potter, 'A Note from Mr Milne', *New Statesman* 91 (1976), p. 548.
12 Ibid., pp. 548–9.

frustratingly vague and reticent about what this reason might be – the quotation in the last paragraph was the entirety of his argument – but with hindsight, his objection to the play becomes clearer.

Brimstone and Treacle deals with intrusion. The essence of the plot is that Martin, pretending to be someone he is not (Pattie's friend and would-be fiancé), and something he is not (the ideal house-trained man, 'mumsy's little helper'), enters the Bates household and, left alone, abuses his position. As such, the play addresses a very ancient human demarcation of space into inside and outside: 'outside' is the jungle, 'inside' a place of safety which is today called 'home'. At one level, then, the conflict is between the civilized values of 'home' and the feral savagery of the outside. Martin is a creature of the latter. Early on, he sneers at the traffic in the street: 'Sick, sick people in metal boxes. They do not know the taste of blood in their mouths. They do not know the glory of the hunt as I know it, as *demons* know it.' (p. 33) Later, he uses Pattie to satisfy humanity's most animal drive, sexual lust. He is dangerous because, unlike the beasts of the jungle, he is intelligent and articulate. 'I can smell the domesticity on your clothes, you sick grey blobs, you timid *mortals*' (p. 32), he says in a scripted line cut from the finished version. His rejection of domesticity, of the 'inside' he seeks to penetrate and disrupt, is conscious and considered: it is something he recognizes well enough to imitate.

Martin brilliantly mimics the petty gentility, the religiosity, the sentimentality, of the environment he enters. 'The plain truth is,' he lies, 'that I once dared to ask Patricia to be my bride' (p. 38), the last word playing up to the romantic fantasies of his suburban middle-class hostess with chilling precision. Accordingly, Mrs Bates – whose greatest pride seems to lie in not using tea-bags or instant coffee – is entirely taken in by this 'nice young man . . . who says his prayers and knows long poems *off by heart*' (p. 46). Her husband is harder to convince. His most revealing domestic trait is that he 'can't stand stains' (p. 37) – a finicky distaste for chaos in the home which reflects a larger fear of intrusion. On the widest scale, his political views are underpinned by the same concern: he has recently left the Conservative Party to join the National Front. Among his worries he lists 'Drugs. Violence. Indiscipline. . . . Strikes. Subversion. Pornography' (p. 49), but his *bête noir* is immigration: 'There'll always be an England. Ha! Not with half the cities full of coloured men, there won't!' (p. 49) He is the archetypal Englishman whose home, even in suburban Archenfield Avenue, is his castle. No wonder he is instinctively suspicious of Martin, even without recognizing him as a kind of immigrant from another metaphysical plane.

The different levels of Mr Bates's concern reflect the concentricity with which the play treats Martin's intrusiveness. The action is structured like a camera zoom as he enters the different degrees of private space. First he bumps into Bates in the street, then (having obtained his address by stealing his wallet) crosses the threshold of his home. The focus on an objective sharpens with the next stage: he is invited to spend the night in Pattie's old bedroom, preserved as she had left it, and he amuses himself by rifling through her underwear and squeezing blood out of a bra. Finally he invades the most private space of all when he rapes Pattie.

Martin is, then, a character who violates boundaries: he resists containment. This is true even of the containment which delimits every character in every play. He has an unnerving habit of looking at the camera – one of the cardinal sins for an actor in realist film and television. It is as if he is the only one who knows he is taking part in a television play, knows that there is an audience watching – us. The impression is confirmed when, just before the first of the two rape scenes, he turns to address the audience directly in sing-song 'Patience Strong' couplets:

> If-you-are-a-nervous-type-out-there,
> Switch-over-or-off-for-cleaner-air.
> But-you-have-to-be-very-smug-or-very-frail
> To-believe-that *no man* has-a-horn-or-tail.   (p. 42)

The perpetrator of the outrage usurps the role of the neutral continuity announcer, warning us that what we are about to see is unsuitable for children or persons of a nervous disposition.

Now we are better placed to understand Alasdair Milne's objection to *Brimstone and Treacle*. Broadcasting has been called 'of its nature both a private and a public practice', and it is this dichotomy which is central to the debate on television censorship.[13] One prevalent BBC philosophy holds that television offers its viewers a 'window on the world' (the phrase comes from the Richard Dimbleby era of *Panorama*), making available aspects of life which lie beyond their everyday experience. But since the days of Lord Reith, the Corporation has also been conscious that its broadcasts, though transmitted through

13 Tracey and Morrison, *Whitehouse*, p. 123.

the public airwaves, are received in a private place, the home, and that this imposes certain standards and conventions: the notorious dinner jackets that Reith's announcers wore behind the microphone were simply the appropriate dress for visiting. Shaun Sutton, who headed the BBC's Television Drama Group in 1976, is quotably succinct in his account of the reasoning as it applied in his field:

> If a play offends it is an assault within the home and its outrage is the greater. Television invades man's privacy to an extent he would not tolerate from friend or neighbour. Drama, traditionally the host of the evening's entertainment, is now the guest in the house. As such, it should assume the graces and responsibilities of a guest.[14]

The feeling that the home was being violated by the intrusion of undesirable broadcast material was the driving force of Mary Whitehouse's campaign, and, drawing in its horns in 1973, the BBC accepted that radio and television drama could not be judged by the same standards as the other media: 'drama to be seen or heard at home must accept restraints which do not necessarily apply to the theatre or the cinema'.[15]

This is one reason why *Brimstone and Treacle* could be printed, staged in a public theatre, and projected onto a cinema screen, but also be considered unsuitable for broadcast television.[16] The other is that much of its impact derives from its being a television play: to have it performed in a public place was an unsatisfactory compromise. To transmit the play, with its sensitive content, into the home could be seen as an enactment of the intrusion it represents in its action. To make matters worse, this intrusion is committed knowingly: when Martin acknowledges the audience, he becomes a presence in the room, looking through at us from the other side of the screen. If television is a window on the world, then *Brimstone and Treacle* seems to deny its viewers the benefit of net curtains.[17]

---

[14] Shaun Sutton, *The Largest Theatre in the World: Thirty Years of Television Drama* (London, 1982), p. 131.

[15] Tracey and Morrison, *Whitehouse*, pp. 197–9; *The Times*, 8 February 1973, p. 4.

[16] It is perhaps relevant that, according to audience research findings, the subject matter which most disturbs television viewers, far more than the portrayal of violence, is the violation of the home, albeit by burglars rather than a visiting demon: Laurie Taylor and Bob Mullan, *Uninvited Guests: The Intimate Secrets of Television and Radio* (London, 1986), p. 55.

[17] It is, of course, ludicrously naive to suppose that Martin is actually inside

It follows, that, in one respect, Milne's judgement was valid: the play would be likely to outrage some of its viewers if broadcast. The next stage of his deliberation, as his letter to Dennis Potter indicates, was to balance that outrage against an assessment of the importance or triviality of the play itself. In this respect he was following the procedure which has been used in obscenity trials since 1959, when the Obscene Publications Act provided for a defence of literary or artistic merit – though he, of course, considered the play in camera and without benefit of expert testimony.

The key issue is the play's objective – in Milne's terms, whether it seeks to make 'a point of serious importance' – and to some extent this is bound up with Martin's objective. Martin is the character through whom we see: we share in his knowledge and ignorance of key information, such as (respectively) the fact that he is not human and the full circumstances of Pattie's accident (known, until the end, only to Pattie and her father). This creates a disturbing impression of complicity, which is enhanced when he glances to camera: by drawing us in like this, he makes us voyeuristic intruders in the household too. Crucially, Martin is given no adequate motive for what he does.[18] The play opens with him searching for bourgeois prey: 'Which one? Which one will it be?' (p. 31) Selection is difficult because it doesn't really matter whom he picks: disruption is an end in itself (he acts for the hell of it, so to speak), and the choice of victim will make only a minor difference in the quality of the aesthetic experience. Martin doesn't need a motive (after all, he's a demon), but *Brimstone and Treacle* does. If we identify his mischief (or anarchism) with the values of the play itself, we must conclude that it is brilliantly and gratuitously offensive (and therefore, in Milne's terms, should be banned).

That is the misjudgement on which, presumably, the decision to withdraw the play was based.[19] It disturbs by showing the invasion of a home, and suggesting the invasion of our own. At a more sophisticated level it disturbs, too, by making us, in our homes, identify more

the television set, in the manner of the cartoons about television that were common in its early days; but this is the ultimate corollary of the belief that the information contained in a broadcast signal can somehow constitute an intrusion. Potter and his director, Barry Davis, play up to this

[18] There is, of course, a sexual motive for the abuse of Pattie, but this emerges in him only after he has entered the house.

[19] It is possible that the play's association with a popular genre, mentioned above, also made it appear trivial.

with the feral Martin than with the domesticated Bates – with viol-
ator rather than victim. But these disturbances are the vehicle for the
point of the play, not the point itself. That point is to question the
mythology of 'home': crossing boundaries is the first step towards
challenging their illusory absoluteness.

Before Martin arrives at Archenfield Avenue, during perhaps the
first fifteen minutes of the action, there is a lot of verbal imagery of
human beings inside enclosed spaces; this helps to establish the play's
concern with inside and outside, home and foreign territory. Some of
these spaces are protective, like the 'metal boxes' (p. 33) which the
rush-hour commuters drive home. What is significant is that more are
claustrophobic and threatening. The idea that Pattie might still be
sentient somewhere inside her body is one that upsets Bates: 'to be
cooped up, inside your own head and be unable to – to –' (p. 34) As
for Mrs Bates, housebound for two years since Pattie cannot be left,
she tells her husband, 'I feel as though I'm scraping my nails on the
lid. . . . The lid of my coffin.' (p. 35) 'Home' has become confining as
well as secure: the absolute dichotomy between the safety of inside
and the danger of outside is already starting to break down.

That dichotomy is the basis of the opposition between Bates and
Martin which is the axis of the drama. As a denizen of that dangerous
outer world, Martin has bestial tendencies which he does his best to
keep hidden in company. Besides his unpleasant sexual propensities,
he is also a sadist, and becomes injudiciously excited during a discussion with Bates of the consequences of National Front policy,
consequences which lead from deportation to concentration camps to
genocide: 'Think of all the *hate* they'll feel! Think of all the violence!
Think of the pain and the degradation and in the end the riots and
the shooting and the –' (p. 50) All this makes Bates first uncomfortable, then repelled, and finally he decides to cancel his National
Front subscription – another case of the demonic man doing good in
spite of himself. But, again, an absolute dichotomy is impossible to
sustain. In an isolated but very striking moment early on, Bates pronounces against the driver who hit Pattie and caused her condition:
'He should be hung up. On a steel rope. . . . All I hope is that whoever
did it dies full of cancer, screaming his head off.' (p. 38) Even allowing
for the understandable vindictiveness of the bereaved, the steel rope is
the product of a sick imagination. It shows that Bates contains the
same nasty streak of sadism that we later see in Martin: it is not so
wide, nor so powerful, but the point is that it is there.

Bates is more overtly concerned with matters of sexual decency. In the past he has disapproved of Pattie's friends, his wife tells Martin, and in particular of Susan, whom he calls 'a slut . . . one of those girls who'll –'. (pp. 47–8) Now, he refuses to go out with his wife for fear that Pattie will expose herself to the babysitter, and he is concerned that Martin's help should not extend to washing or changing her: 'Her brain may be damaged. But her body is that of an attractive young woman.' (p. 46) Martin puts his finger on it brilliantly when he summarizes, as if offended: 'He means that it would be *indecent* for me to see her poor, helpless body, *obscene* for me to help make her more comfortable, and *lewd* and disgusting to – to –'. (p. 46) Mrs Bates is not far from the truth when, responding to this prompt, she rounds on her husband and accuses him of filthy thoughts – even though she is wrong to go on to say that such thoughts would never enter Martin's head. For if in Martin sexuality is rampant, in Bates it is not absent but merely repressed.[20]

Bates is exposed as a corollary of Pattie's recovery, and this gives us the hindsight to see that his despair of that recovery, expressed throughout the play in marked contrast with his wife's optimism, was in part a form of repressed hope. Martin is the unwitting agent of this exposure in raping Pattie into articulate consciousness. This is not just a somewhat unorthodox form of shock therapy: it is a brutal reminder of the circumstances which led up to the accident in the first place – which is why both rape scenes induce flashbacks to that event. It becomes clear in the final moments of the play that Pattie ran out into the road after finding her father in bed with her friend Susan. Her mental incapacity has been the invisible keystone of the Bates household, ensuring her silence about the home-wrecking adultery she has witnessed.

In short, the difference between Martin and Bates is one of degree, not antithesis, and this has implications for Bates's isolationist philosophy as a whole. Not only is it politically undesirable at its widest dilation, it is also based on a fallacy: the things that he tries to keep outside, the wild, savage traits that give Martin his true identity, are already inside, at the centre of the home he wishes to protect. At the deepest level of enclosed space, within his own psyche, the binary

---

[20] This aspect is further enhanced in the 1982 film's version of the underwear-rifling sequence. Here the representation of Martin's actions is ambiguated by being integrated with shots of Bates suffering a nightmare; we later learn, in dialogue unique to this version, that he has himself been caught 'inspecting' Pattie's underwear.

distinctions of inside and outside, civilization and savagery, man and beast, collapse into one another.

The development of the play, then, is away from the disconcerting surprise which, at first, we are induced to feel as we are made to see things through Martin rather than through Bates. That initial discomfort arises partly from our preconceptions about the moral nature of Martin's actions, but also from our awareness that Bates belongs to the same home environment in which we sit watching the play: he is the one we feel we should identify with, and are not allowed to. But by the end of the play, such feelings have become irrelevant.

So far I have argued that this irrelevance follows from the play's skepticism about the privileged status of home space compared with outside, and its resistance of binary oppositions between the two. But not all viewers are so responsive, or so sympathetic: some may find the entire play irrelevant, either through lack of interest or (more importantly here) through hostility. In revealing the similarity that underlies the seeming antithesis between Martin and Bates, *Brimstone and Treacle* asks a disturbing question about our own pretensions to civilization. This is the crucial point in the censorship process. Viewers who cannot face that question will operate a personal censor mechanism which enables them to discard the play: to them it becomes trivial, or nauseating, or outrageous, a programme unfit for broadcasting. It only takes a position of power for an individual to turn his personal, psychological act of censorship into an institutional ban.

That there is such a connection between censorship and repression is evinced by the difficulty of establishing in specific terms what it is in a work's content that will cause it to be banned, or prosecuted.[21] Advocates and practitioners of censorship tend to prefer imprecise pejorative terms like 'filth', which save them from having to engage with the nature of the material they seek to suppress. Even the keystone of English legal censorship, the concept of 'obscenity', has been defined since 1868 as a 'tendency . . . to deprave and corrupt', without any apparent need to establish what depravity and corruption might be.[22] Subjective terms 'define' one another in a meaningless hall of mirrors: juries who convict in censorship cases may not know much

[21] An exception is the Video Recordings Act 1984, which specifies in section 2 (2) some of the subject matter within its ambit; it is the only English legal instrument of censorship which does so.

[22] *Law Reports* 3, Queen's Bench Division (1867–8), p. 371. For a more detailed discussion of the impossibility of defining obscenity, see George

about obscenity, but they know what they don't like. Or rather, they know it when they see it, for censorship, whether personal, institutional, or public, is very much an *ad hoc* practice. Because there are no precise rules, only a body of case law, it is not always possible to foresee trouble with the censor, as the BBC Drama Group found out in 1976.

This is, of course, a very one-sided account: one might put it differently by saying that censorship is a reactive rather than a proactive phenomenon, incited by a work's transgression of boundaries, albeit sometimes ill-defined ones. The process is itself part of the effort of definition: material is suppressed when (with whatever degree of intelligence or articulacy) it reminds us of the relativity of principles which we should prefer to think of as absolute. Usually this serves to afford a degree of legal or institutional protection to culturally sensitive ideas; in modern Britain, the censor is called upon to defend from question and challenge beliefs about such things as sex, religion, and the innocence of childhood. The paradox is that, to its supporters, censorship may itself be an absolute to be protected by these means, and in a sense this was the root of *Brimstone and Treacle*'s troubles at the BBC.

This is not to say that the play deals directly with censorship – patently it does not, and in practice to ban such a play would anyway have been too embarrassing to contemplate – but in Bates it presents a prime example of the censorship mentality. His concern to keep his household undefiled, to make it a privileged space by means which the play identifies as psychological repression, is a physical correlative for the censorship process in general, and an exact analogy with the ideas used to defend television censorship in particular. As Potter had recognized, the suburban setting of Archenfield Avenue is typical 'National Viewers' and Listeners' Association' territory. 'Potter . . . loves the idea of Mrs Whitehouse,' wrote a *Guardian* interviewer in 1973. 'He sees her as standing up for all the people with ducks on their walls who have been laughed at and treated like rubbish by the sophisticated metropolitan minority.'[23] The ducks on the wall are an especially telling detail. No doubt it would be in such households, so like that of Mr and Mrs Bates, that the transmission of *Brimstone and Treacle* would have provoked the greatest outrage: in challenging the

Ryley Scott, *Into Whose Hands: An Examination of Obscene Libel in its Legal, Sociological and Literary Aspects* (London, 1945), pp. 25–7.
[23] Stanley Reynolds, *The Guardian*, 16 February 1973, p. 10.

sanctity of the home, the play calls into question the fundamental principles of the advocates of television censorship; to them, more than anyone else, *Brimstone and Treacle* would have seemed eminently censorable.

The play glances briefly at its own exclusion from the airwaves when Bates remarks that he has bought his wife a colour television.[24] Martin promptly starts a conversation about *Songs of Praise* – the epitome of 'wholesome' television to the advocates of programming suitable for viewing at home (meaning a suburban, middle-class, ducks-on-wall home). What concerned Potter about the BBC's mid-1970s trend towards a tighter control of broadcast content was that its output might become restricted to such programmes. Not long after *Brimstone and Treacle* was accepted for production, he wrote in *The Observer*:

> The [late nineteenth-century] theatre was waiting for something like moving pictures to go down into the nightmares of dislocation and unease which both scar and ennoble modern man. The television play has this freedom, and it is seriously threatened at the moment precisely because its stumbling innovations and infant awkwardness are seen by the programme planners as disturbances, which mix ill with the treacle of TV entertainment or the 'balanced' editing of TV journalism.[25]

In the play, the irony is that Bates has bought the television set to enable his housebound wife to get out vicariously. In practice, however, all the 'window on the world' lets into their home is more of its own stuffy atmosphere, in the form of *Songs of Praise* and its ilk: the sort of 'treacle' which, Potter argued, gums up a medium which could be used for serious, challenging plays. In acting to protect Britain's ducks-on-wall homes from such a play, Alasdair Milne simply proved the thesis.[26]

---

[24] Understandably, this moment assumed greater importance when Potter adapted the play for the stage: in this version (p. 12), Martin gives another of his significant looks to the audience at the mention of the television set, which is highlighted in the opening stage direction as 'the only brand-new, or brazenly modern piece of furniture' in the room (p. 1). The television script contains neither of these details.

[25] 'Dennis Potter on the Challenge of TV Drama', *Observer* colour supplement, 27 April 1975, p. 23.

[26] I am grateful to Nick Cooper for his help in researching this essay.

Notes on Contributors

Jonathan Bate is King Alfred Professor of English Literature at the University of Liverpool. He is the author of *Shakespeare and the English Romantic Imagination* (Oxford, 1986), *Shakespearean Constitutions: Politics, Theatre, Criticism 1730–1830* (Oxford, 1989), and *Romantic Ecology* (Routledge, 1991); he has also edited an anthology, *The Romantics on Shakespeare*, for Penguin (1992).

Joseph Bristow is Lecturer in English Literature at the University of York. His publications include *Empire Boys: Adventures in a Man's World* (Harper Collins, 1991) and *Robert Browning* (Brighton, 1991). He is the editor of *Sexual Sameness: Textual Difference in Lesbian and Gay Writing* (Routledge, 1992), is currently writing *Effeminate England: Homosexual Writing and National Identity 1885–1985* (Open University Press, Gender and Writing series), and editing the *Oxford Book of Adventure Stories*.

Kate Flint is University Lecturer in Victorian and Modern English Literature, University of Oxford, and a Fellow of Linacre College. Her publications include *Dickens* (Brighton, 1986) and *The Woman Reader, 1837–1914* (Oxford, 1993). She is currently engaged in a study of the imaginative function of fluids in Victorian culture.

Paul Hammond is Lecturer in English at the University of Leeds. He is the author of *John Oldham and the Renewal of Classical Culture* (Cambridge, 1983) and *John Dryden: A Literary Life* (Macmillan, 1992). He is also the editor of the *Selected Prose of Alexander Pope* (Cambridge, 1987), and the forthcoming edition of the poems of John Dryden in the Longman Annotated English Poets series.

Jon Mee is Lecturer in English Literature at the Australian National University, Canberra. He is the author of *Dangerous Enthusiasm: William Blake and the Culture of Radicalism in the 1790s* (Oxford, 1992).

Lucasta Miller studied English and Renaissance Studies at the Universities of Oxford and London. She is currently writing a study of the Brontë myth in popular culture.

Martin Wiggins is a Fellow of the Shakespeare Institute, University of Birmingham, and the author of several articles on Shakespeare's tragedies and *Journeymen in Murder: The Assassin in English Renaissance Drama* (Oxford, 1991). He is also one of the general editors of the forthcoming Oxford World's Classics Drama Library.

Richard Wilson is Lecturer in English at the University of Lancaster, and the author of *Will Power: Essays on Shakespearean authority* (Hemel Hempstead, 1993). He has written the volume on *Julius Caesar* (Harmondsworth, 1992 in the Penguin Critical Studies Series, and edited Longman Critical Readers on *New Historicism and Renaissance Drama* (London, 1992) and *Christopher Marlowe* (London, 1993).